BLACK TAX

Edited by Niq Mhlongo

Jonathan Ball Publishers
Johannesburg & Cape Town

Originally published in South Africa in 2019 by
JONATHAN BALL PUBLISHERS
A division of Media24 (Pty) Ltd
PO Box 33977
Jeppestown
2043

ISBN 9781868429745
ebook ISBN 9781868429752

Every effort has been made to trace the copyright holders and to obtain their permission for the use of copyright material. The publishers apologise for any errors or omissions and would be grateful to be notified of any corrections that should be incorporated in future editions of this book.

Twitter: www.twitter.com/JonathanBallPub
Facebook: www.facebook.com/JonathanBallPublishers
Blog: http://jonathanball.bookslive.co.za/

Cover by Johan Koortzen
Design and typesetting by Nazli Jacobs
Editing by Katlego Tapala
Proofreading by Paul Wise
Printed and bound by CTP Printers, Cape Town
Set in Sabon

Contents

Introduction

'Black tax' is a highly sensitive and complex topic that is often debated among black South Africans. While these debates are always inconclusive due to the ambiguity, irony and paradoxes that surround it, as black people we all agree that 'black tax' is part of our daily lives.

This book acknowledges these complexities and tries to represent a vast variety of voices on this subject. In the process of compiling these essays, I therefore specifically tried to get a diversity of viewpoints by incorporating young and old, urban and rural, male and female contributors.

The main question posed in the book is whether 'black tax' is a burden or a blessing. Is it indeed some kind of tax or an act of ubuntu? The essays in this book represent both views.

In an attempt to answer this question, the idea of both the black family and the black middle class are interrogated. The point is made that as an ideological concept the black family is constantly changing to accommodate new economic, political and social realities and opportunities.

While some refer to black managers, government officials, professionals like teachers and nurses, academics and clerks as the black middle class, some contributors take issue with this categorisation. According to them there is no black middle class in South Africa, only poverty masked by graduation gowns and debts. 'Black tax' therefore affects every black person and not only a particular class because we are all taxed and surviving on revolving credit.

The term 'black tax' also isn't acceptable to all. Many people take issue with it and say it should not be labelled as a kind of tax, but should be called something else, like family responsibility. According to this viewpoint, we need to investigate and politicise the historical roots of black tax by viewing it in the context of a racialised, apartheid South Africa.

Apartheid is seen as a system that socially engineered black poverty and loss of land for black people. This meant that black South Africans couldn't build generational wealth. After apartheid, the capitalist system perpetuated these inequalities. For example, a black person may earn the same salary as their white counterparts, but they will have more financial responsibilities to their family, which is often still trapped in poverty due to the inequalities that were engineered by the apartheid system.

The above perspective stands in opposition to those who say that 'black tax' is an undeniable part of black culture and the African way of living according to the philosophy of ubuntu. A number of contributors write positively about how much they have benefited from so-called black tax and how much joy they get from being able to give back once they start earning.

Then there is also the viewpoint that links 'black tax' to the place and role of the ancestors. To look after family members is to keep the spirit of the ancestors alive and to ensure continuity between the past and the present. It keeps the black family intact.

Some authors therefore believe this way of life is something black South Africans should be proud of.

The one thing the contributors seem to agree on is that black tax is a daily reality for nearly every black South African, from sons and daughters who build homes for their parents to brothers and sisters who put siblings through school, and to the student who diverts bursary money to put food on the table back home. There are also several moving stories that refer to how people would simply open their homes to near and distant family, or even relative strangers, in need of help or a place to stay.

My personal observation is that most black people become breadwinners at an early age, some even at 18, and are then expected to be 'deputy parents'. The moment we start earning we are seen as 'messiahs' who will rescue the family from poverty.

One especially sad theme that this collection brings to light is the dashed hopes of youngsters who aren't allowed to study within the fields they are passionate about. Black parents expect their children to study something that will allow them to earn a high salary one day.

Linked to this are the deferred dreams of so many people who put their family commitments before their own needs. For instance, one of the contributors mentions how he couldn't continue with his postgraduate studies because he first had to put his siblings through school.

A number of stories are testament to the resilience of the human spirit in their descriptions of grandmothers and mothers who assume the role of paterfamilias and ensure their family's survival despite grinding poverty. Inadvertently, this adds to the debate over how black women are suffering doubly as a result of patriarchy and the demands imposed upon them by black tax.

When reading the contributions, it also becomes clear that many people feel conflicted about 'black tax'. They point to some of its negative aspects, like people who fall into debt to keep up with their family's expectations. They also describe the guilt trips they are put on, not only by their parents or family, but also by pastors and other church officials.

Sadly, there are also those who expect handouts and/or waste whatever is given to them on frivolous things. One contributor even goes so far as to describe a family's unrelenting demands as 'predatory'. This is one of the challenges posed by black tax and to me it is also symbolic of the rise and decline of the black family as a social entity.

Many South African middle-class-income households are connected to working-class families. In the context of hunger and poverty it becomes unavoidable to send money home. Therefore, the point is made that the only way the issue of 'black tax' can be addressed is to solve the problem of inequality in the country and to challenge class identity.

Many contributors feel that by paying 'black tax' they are taking over what is essentially supposed to be a government responsibility. They call black tax an alternative form of social security. The government, they contend, has a duty to address South Africa's economic challenges of the past through affirmative action and decent education and by creating jobs.

In fact, 'black tax' can be seen as a form of income redistribution. Given its prevalence and influence, I think that black tax has a great impact on our economy. Thousands of people would be even worse off if it wasn't for their employed family members helping them out.

For all these reasons, I'm surprised it doesn't get greater official recognition, by government for instance and also in public debate.

The real significance of this book lies in the fact that it tells us more about the everyday life of black South Africans. It delves into the essence of black family life and the secret anguish of family members who often battle to cope.

In reading this book, I hope that most readers will be able to share in the pain and joy and reflect on our lives as black people. My great wish is that it will offer a better understanding of the social, economic and political organisation of those affected by 'black tax'.

I see this book as an opportunity to start a necessary dialogue among black South Africans about this aspect of our reality. It is clear that the majority of us have come to the point where this social and economic responsibility can no longer be viewed merely as a part of culture. We no longer want to be trapped within the confines of 'black tax'.

I'm extremely grateful to all the contributors who came on board and helped me to compile this important book within five months. Each of them was keen to write something on the topic, which they believe deserves further exploration. I'm grateful for the depth of the contributions and the valuable insights they offer into the social, political and economic debate around 'black tax'.

It takes individuals of rare ability, courage, dedication and vision to tap into private memories and then lay them bare for public scrutiny. I cannot thank you enough.

Niq Mhlongo
Meadowlands, Soweto

PART 1

Black tax – what you give up and what you gain

Dudu Busani-Dube

I was going to try and humour you, until I realised, I had no right.

I was going to tell you about my petty 'black tax' experiences which, after I had sat down and thought about, I found more funny than frustrating. I was going to tell you about the many times I've gone to fetch my mother from church and ended up with four of her mates on my back seat whom I've had to drop off at their houses, spread across the whole township of KwaMashu. One of them might want to pass by the local Shoprite to buy something while the others wait in my car with their arms folded, firing off questions like when am I having a baby and am I taking good care of my husband.

Where I come from, everyone old enough to be your parent is your parent. They also raised you and saying no to them is not an option, which is why you pay your black tax without whining, whether it is by emptying your petrol tank driving them around or accommodating their children in your house when they come to Joburg for job interviews.

I was going to tell you how, even though my parents have a three-bedroomed house and only my brother and I lived with them – though we were five children in total – I never had my own bedroom. I assume that when they bought the house, they figured it was going to be big enough for their small family with their bedroom, my bedroom and my brother's bedroom but no . . . that turned out to be a far-fetched dream.

For as long as I can remember, my parents' house was always some kind of 'halfway house' where every family member – immediate or extended – could stop and stay while trying to find their feet in Durban. There were also children of neighbours, from the village where my father was born, who passed through; some from my mother's side of the family and, at one point, a woman called Eggy, from Lesotho. I still don't know what that was about.

Most of these people have gone on to become something in life. Today, many own even bigger houses than my parents'. So it dawned on me that my parents have been paying black tax from before I was born. Only, in their time it was about 'breaking the cycle'.

I wasn't sure about my contribution to 'breaking the cycle' and it bothered me, so I called my father, a 64-year-old retired primary school principal, who shocked us seven years ago when he announced he was retiring at 57.

'I'm tired,' he simply said when asked about his reasons.

When he made the announcement, my brother was 23 and already grown-up and I had also been working for years, so a part of me understood why father was tired. I have always known he had a difficult life growing up. He had seven siblings of whom he was the second eldest.

When I called him, I asked him a few basic questions like, 'Baba, what was the first thing you did for khulu when you started working?'

'You mean when I was ten years old?' he asked.

I was climbing trees and eating bread with jam when I was ten, so his question didn't make sense to me. 'No, when you started teaching at your first school in Mzinyathi,' I said.

He explained to me that, actually, his first job was somewhere in Stanger when he was about nine years old. He worked for a white man without knowing what his specific job description was, he just did as he was told.

I didn't know this.

I also didn't know that he only started school when he was ten and that, while going to school, he worked at the village hospital on weekends, where he earned 25c a week.

'With the money I made, your grandmother bought a goat and that goat had lambs and that's how we got to have livestock.'

I remember there were goats at my grandmother's house in the five-year period during which I lived there as a child. There was a house, too, which we called 'endlini enkulu'. It was a mud house, but it had a good shape and on the inside there was a set of sofas, a table and dining room chairs.

'We built that house when I started working, with the salary I earned in the first three months. It was three hundred and something, I was earning R125 a month.'

The 'we' includes his late elder brother, who didn't go further than lower primary school because he was the eldest and had to work to support the family.

I wanted him to tell me more, but I could feel him withdrawing. He ended the conversation with 'Ayixoxeki le, but it made us men.'

My father, being of an older generation, wasn't familiar with the term 'black tax' and heard it for the first time during our conversation. This, of course, is very telling. I found that I could not explain it to him, lest he found it offensive because to him helping others was a responsibility, something that automatically came with being an elder sibling. I feel equally uncomfortable with this term.

My father made it to a teaching college with the assistance of the Lutheran church and was appointed principal before he turned 35. Judging by what he had to go through to get there, he was very successful, and in our community, success comes with expectations, it comes with the responsibility to send the elevator back down to fetch the others.

After hearing my father's story, a part of me still wanted to whine a little bit about black tax and how it isn't really necessary in this day and age. After all, aren't we out of the dark ages now, with opportunities available to everyone?

And so, I found myself having this conversation with my elder sister, the daughter of my father's brother, who has made my life very difficult by doing everything right and instilling in me a fear of failure. When I mentioned black tax, she said, 'Weeeeeeeh, you should have prepared me for this.'

I couldn't see her at the other end of the line, but I could picture her with her hands over her head as she said this. She is the eldest of the more than 25 grandchildren – the loudest, the feistiest and also the one who fully understands the poverty our family comes from and has carried it on her shoulders since she was a child.

There wasn't any money for her to go to university, brilliant as she was, and so she waited two years before she was accepted into a government nursing school which afforded her an opportunity to do her degree at the University of Zululand.

She immediately sent the elevator back down with the R1 800 student-nurse stipend.

First, you take care of home. That's a rule of black families that doesn't need to be written down. She built a two-bedroomed brick house for her mother, opened an Ellerines credit account and bought the first sofas and a fridge. She told me this without an ounce of bitterness in her tone. I didn't understand how.

While the rest of the adults in our family were taking care of everyone else, she was taking care of me and her younger siblings. To me, she was my sister with a job, and that meant I could get clothes from her. Her student residence at the hospital was where I went for vacation during school holidays. The best time of my life because I could sit around doing nothing all day and eat as much as I wanted, while she was out studying during the day and sometimes working at night.

Now we go on holidays together, dine in fine restaurants and steal each other's clothes, but the subject of how much we delayed her journey to such a life never comes up. We don't need her money anymore, but where would we be without the R1 800 she had to split amongst us?

In the same vein, where would those many people be had my parents closed their doors to them and decided it's each man for himself?

Black tax is a sensitive subject. We are not prepared to explain it to people who can never understand the depth of it and we never will, just ask that other bank that once tried us on this matter. This is also why we black people can joke about it, but will immediately go into attack mode if a white person even tries to join the conversation; because *we* are the children of domestic workers and gardeners, we have no 'old money' and nothing to inherit.

It comes with some anger, too, and no, it is not directed at the families we have to take care of, but at the system that was created to ensure that no matter how much freedom we think we finally have, it will still take us decades to crawl out of the dungeon we were thrown in.

We still laugh about it, though, just like we laugh about land, sometimes.

Black tax isn't our culture, no, it isn't. It has everything to do with the position this country's history has put us in. It is not even entirely about money. It begins with the sacrifices we have to make because of a lack of money.

Black tax is being a 19-year-old varsity student at res, with nothing to eat, but then not calling home to ask for money because you know there isn't any.

Black tax is earning a big enough salary to buy your first car, but you can't because the bank loan you took to fix your parents' dilapidated house landed you at the credit bureau.

Black tax is not having an option to take a gap year after matric because what is that, anyway?

Black tax is opting to go for a diploma when you qualify for a degree, because a diploma takes only three years, and hopefully you'll get a job after that and take over paying your siblings' school fees so that your mother can maybe quit her job at that horrible family she is working for in the suburbs.

Black tax is understanding that you can't stay at varsity full-time to do your honours and master's because NSFAS (the

National Student Financial Aid Scheme) might not pay for it.

Black tax is the anxiety you have before a job interview because your township-school English might just humiliate you and cost you a career opportunity.

Black tax is being in Johannesburg and trying very hard to hide your struggles from your family back in Mtubatuba, or Qonce, because you don't want them to worry.

Black tax is your mother having to change the subject every time the neighbours ask her why her paint is peeling and her geyser broken when she has an employed daughter.

Black tax is all the shit that plunges us into depression and forces some of us to live a lie.

It's not our parents' fault, they had it even worse. They fought and died and paid their fair share to get us to where we are. Most of them never even ask for the things we offer them.

Black tax is also the biggest enemy of marriage and a source of sibling rivalry. Some of us enter marriage carrying large financial responsibilities on our shoulders. Just think about it, what happens if you marry a man whose financial success was made possible by an elder sibling's sacrifice? Or if you marry a woman who was put through school by an uncle who worked in the mines and was a breadwinner, with the hope that one day she would take the weight off his shoulders so he could go off to start his own family?

Imagine being a newlywed with plans of buying your new home and having as many children as you want, only to find almost half of your new spouse's earnings go to supporting his or her family. It's an unspoken debt, and usually the reason why a family meeting can never start without S'bongile but can continue without S'lindile.

The thing is, S'bongile 'has money' – she renovated and extended the family house and Christmas lunch wouldn't happen without her. S'lindile still lives in that same family house and dropped out of school when she fell pregnant and now has three children with different deadbeat fathers. Every month, S'lindile queues for the government child-support grant and buys a couple of bags of rice and a braai pack, but nobody notices or thanks her, because S'bongile's groceries arrive in a bakkie, with trays of lamb, boxes of cornflakes and 100 per cent fruit juice.

S'lindile can't stand S'bongile because everyone treats her like she's better. S'bongile resents S'lindile because every month she has to fork out money so S'lindile's three children can eat, even though she wishes she had a bigger TV and a more comfortable bed in her flat, where towards the end of the month, her supper is two-minute noodles. S'bongile might want to get out of this arrangement and focus on herself, but her conscience won't let her forget that without S'lindile, there would be nobody staying at home to take care of their elderly mother; there would be no functioning, warm home to go back to.

While I personally do not relate to S'lindile – even though to an extent I am a beneficiary of black tax – S'bongile is more like many people my age that I come across daily. When I asked for some opinions on my Facebook page, I got a number of strong responses, like the following:

'I don't mind taking care of my mom and grandma, but I feel like the number of stomachs to fill is increasing. I'm slowly getting depressed because people just consume, consume and consume. No one is coming with a side hustle or a way to assist me. I spend more than R3 000 on food and I don't even eat most of it.

'I'm tired. If I had no black tax to pay, I would have my second degree and a house. Black tax is making it hard for us to realise our dreams, especially when you earn peanuts. Ke lapile, I feel like running away from home.'

I got her, I really did get her frustration, but I also understood the conflicting responses to her comment. 'Calling helping out at home "tax" is just wrong,' one woman wrote. 'It's the reason most people see it as a burden, because we all wish we didn't have to pay taxes. I see no problem in helping out a parent who has done so much for you and now can't afford expenses of living. Phela, had she/he not taken you to school she would probably still afford a life she/he wants. Helping out has to be a choice, neither one of the parents should force it on you. I just don't see how someone sleeps at night living a luxurious life while his parents are barely surviving.'

The fact of the matter is that we – the people who are tasked with the responsibility of breaking the cycle of poverty in the black community in this country – are conflicted on the subject. Nobody has really come out and said this is our responsibility, but we know it is.

For this reason, you tolerate horrible bosses, pretend racism in the workplace isn't an issue and sometimes laugh off sexual harassment in the office because you are just trying to survive and provide. It is also why you often find yourself unwillingly joining one of the pyramid schemes your aunt or uncle is desperately trying to recruit everyone into, because you know they are trying to hustle for their children.

Sometimes it's the guilt that drives you to pay a slightly bigger contribution towards a family funeral than others, or makes you delay announcing to the family WhatsApp group that you've bought yourself a new, luxurious car. It's guilt that makes you tell your children to leave their bikes and play-stations behind when going to a family gathering where there will be nieces and nephews whose mother is a S'lindile.

See, while our freedom might have come with the ability to go where you want, whenever you want and to say what you want, it didn't come with a 'poverty escape plan'. The rest we were left to do ourselves, and unless we do it now, our children and our children's children will still be carrying the burden after we die.

My paternal grandmother, who never set foot in school and couldn't read or write until the day she died, raised children who became teachers and nurses. Her children's children became engineers, nurses, journalists and land surveyors, to name but a few professions. Me and my siblings and cousins are raising children who can be anything they want to be; they are liberals and feminists, creatives and geniuses, travellers and home-makers. They are queer and open-minded, they are fearless and headstrong, innovators and entrepreneurs. These are things that would never have been possible had my parents, uncles and aunts not made the sacrifices they made for each other.

Yes, sometimes looking after your family means you'll be driving on your reserve tank for two days before payday. But really, it's about watching your little brother dressing up for his graduation and your sister starting a business. It's your uncle's bragging rights in the shebeen about the new aluminium gate you had installed at his house.

It's about how everyone comes out to ululate when that furniture shop truck delivers the new leather sofas and your mother covers them with plastic for years while ordering the grandkids to sit on the floor because she doesn't want them to be messed up. Those sofas are precious, because her daughter bought them for her.

It may not make up for the missed trips to Dubai with your friends or the fact that you could have a PhD by now, but maybe the fact that you've changed your family's socio-economic status isn't such a bad thing after all.

DUDU BUSANI-DUBE is a South African fiction writer and a journalist by profession. She has published four novels, including the best-selling *Hlomu* series. In 2018, the 37-year-old was recognised by the Ethekwini Municipality for being among 18 young top achievers from KwaZulu-Natal province. Dudu published her first book in 2014.

An inevitable growing pain

Fred Khumalo

A few years ago, my sister-in-law introduced me to her friend, who, at 25, had just finished her master's degree and was coming to me for help.

I said, 'If you are looking for a job in the media, I could possibly help, but seeing that you are into marketing, I am stumped.'

'No, Bra Fred!' she said, shocked at my assumption, 'I am not looking for a job. I was just wondering if I should perhaps go ahead and do my PhD, or if I should take the next year off, you know, so I could travel overseas and stuff.'

My armpits sweated; my ears itched; my lips trembled. A number of expletives rose to the tip of my tongue: what had this narcissistic nincompoop just said? This contumelious flibbertigibbet was poking fun at me! Her dilemma was whether she should do her PhD or travel overseas? And she was only 25. And she was black!

But then I had to calm down, look at Thandi's reality objectively. I had to remember that she was an only child, and her mother was a single parent who had gone to university – and carved out her own path, independent of a male partner or an extended family.

I had to remember that, though black like myself, she was a child of the 2000s – born after 1994, raised in Cape Town and lucky enough to have imbibed her education from some top Model C schools in that city, after which she progressed to the University of Cape Town; all of this through her mother's efforts.

My reality, on the other hand, was starkly different from this. To appreciate my story, we have to claw back to the mid-1960s.

At the height of apartheid, my father, lucky enough to have obtained a special pass which allowed him to go and look for work in the city, left his village in rural Ixopo, immortalised by Alan Paton in his classic, *Cry, The Beloved Country*. Because he did not have much of an education – only three years of formal schooling – he could not readily find steady employment in Pinetown, the town he settled in, just north-west of Durban.

He worked on construction sites, as a messenger, a 'garden boy' – in those days there were no black men in South Africa, only boys; even if they were 69 years of age, they were boys to the white person – and ultimately as a horse groom. It was during his tenure as a horse groom at Summerveld stables, just outside Pinetown, that he met the woman who would become my mother.

Unlike my father, the woman who would become my mother had left her home township of Chesterville, five minutes from Durban, armed with a Junior Certificate (in today's terms, Grade 10). She had just registered as a trainee nurse at Mariannhill Hospital when she met my father.

They fell in love. I was conceived. My mother dropped out of nursing school. They got married.

A year later, they were given a house of their own in the newly founded Mpumalanga township, just outside the Hammarsdale industrial area, in the Natal midlands. This is where I grew up and went to school. By the time I finished matric, there were eight of us children at home.

My father, who had started out as a smelly horse groom, now held down a respectable job as a tanner at Bata Shoes; my mother, who'd dropped out of nursing school, worked at the same factory as a machinist.

Though my parents were seemingly more respectable than some of our neighbours who still worked on construction sites and as rubbish collectors, with eight children they were clearly struggling financially. The ten of us, eight children and our parents, lived in a two-bedroomed government-issue house.

Inevitably, there were always aunties and uncles and cousins of cousins removed, coming from the rural areas, who would stay with us for a month or two. They used our home as a transit camp while they looked for work in the city, and also tried to find their own lodgings.

That was the reality of most black people in the urban areas. You were always part of a bigger extended family. In later years I would discover that some of these people I'd been told were aunts or uncles were actually not my blood. They just happened to have originated from my father's village in Ixopo. In that way, they were 'family'.

Later in life, I would observe this stretching of familial ties in Italian movies where, upon arriving in America, Italians suddenly became 'relatives' by virtue of the fact that they'd originated from the same village back in Sicily or Palermo.

I'd always known that there was not much money at home.

We were one of the few families in our neighbourhood who couldn't afford to install electricity in our house. In those days it was incumbent upon a homeowner to install electricity in their home, at their own expense.

The government only provided you with an empty four-roomed house – two bedrooms, one kitchen, one living-room-cum-dining-room. The walls were not plastered. There was no ceramic bathtub in the bathroom, no sink in the kitchen. And certainly no electricity.

But the fact that we were penurious registered with me most rudely after I'd finished matric. Confident that I would do well in my final exams, I'd applied at a number of universities around the country. I got accepted at three of them. When our matric results were released, I was thrilled to discover I had obtained a university entrance.

Now came the crunch: there was no money to send me to university. For days I cried. At the last minute, just when schools were about to reopen, my father – who'd gone visiting his ancestral home of Ixopo during the festive season – came back with the news that there was, after all, money for me to proceed with my tertiary studies.

It was up to me to choose which university I wanted to go to. The University of Zululand, which had accepted me, was ruled out; this after students were massacred by armed hordes murdering people under the auspices of Inkatha Yenkululeko Yesizwe, later renamed the Inkatha Freedom Party.

Fort Hare, which had also accepted me, was ruled out simply because transport to the distant Eastern Cape town of Alice was deemed expensive. So, I settled for Technikon Natal, which was then a white college.

Years later, when I'd settled at the technikon, I casually asked my parents how they'd almost overnight managed to raise money to send me to school. What emerged was a story reminiscent of a scene in a novel I'd just finished reading at the time, Chinua Achebe's *No Longer at Ease*, a sequel to his internationally acclaimed classic, *Things Fall Apart*.

In *No Longer at Ease*, when Obi Okonkwo finishes his schooling in the village of Umuofia, in Igboland, Nigeria, it takes the financial support of his fellow villagers to send him to university in England. When he returns, he is not expected to pay the money back; but simply to help others in need.

Without me knowing, this is what had happened to me. My father had gone back to his ancestral village and laid the matter on the table.

Villagers, some of whom had never met me, dug into their back pockets and fished out some coins and banknotes. The bulk of the money, however, came from my paternal aunt, my father's elder sister.

I was stunned speechless as I listened to this story. As if reading my thoughts, my father explained that I was not supposed to pay the money back as it was not a loan; all that was expected of me was, once I had finished my studies, to extend help to those who needed it – to members of my immediate and extended family.

Which is why, upon finishing my National Diploma in Journalism, I felt pressured to go and look for work. So that I could begin ploughing back.

You will recall that there were seven younger siblings of mine, all waiting in the queue so they, too, could go and drink from the fountain of knowledge at tertiary institutions. This, in addition to a very big Khumalo family – aunts, uncles and their children – who were all looking up to me as I was the first in the larger Khumalo family to obtain a tertiary qualification.

Dreams of further education – honours and doctoral degrees – had to be kept in abeyance.

This, in a nutshell, is the harsh reality of what has come to be referred to as black tax. Sometimes, and especially if you are a senior member of the family, you have to defer your dreams in order to accommodate the immediate and pressing needs of others within your orbit.

But, of course, other people, even when they have obtained the financial and moral support of their clan, will steadfastly refuse to remember that. With their first pay, they will buy a car and run off to the city, to lose themselves in the town houses where they will live big, unencumbered by memories of kith and kin.

Charles Dickens had these kinds of people in mind when he wrote: 'Conscience is an elastic and very flexible article, which will bear a deal of stretching and adapt itself to a great variety of circumstances. Some people by prudent management and leaving it off piece by piece like a flannel waistcoat in warm weather, even contrive, in time, to dispense with it altogether; but there be others who can assume the garment and throw it off at pleasure; and this, being the greatest and most convenient improvement, is the one in vogue.'

I know I speak for many when I say that, with our first salaries, those of us who are still equally in touch with both our extended families and our consciences, will either demolish the shack our parents live in and build a proper house, or extend the existing government-issue four-roomed house into something bigger, something more liveable.

A friend of mine, originally from Nelspruit (now referred to as Mbombela), tells an interesting story about his own father. Because his father and his brothers did not have much of an education, they were condemned to go and work on the mines, chasing after that elusive yellow stone that made white people rich, and black people perpetually under-educated and therefore dependent on white benefactors.

Unlike his brothers, who spent their measly wages entertaining themselves on the mines or obtaining wives – polygamy was rife in their rural village – the friend's father spent his money on finishing high school by correspondence. After this, he quit the mines and found a job with an insurance company in Johannesburg. A rung up the ladder of progress.

In the meantime, he built his wife and children a decent home, in their ancestral village, in Nelspruit. It was around this time – faced with the man's big, new house – that his brothers' wives and children started accusing the man of 'bewitching' them so that only he and his immediate family could succeed.

That's right, folks, that's another uniquely black challenge: the belief that if you are not successful there must be someone, especially in your extended family, who is bewitching you. In ancient Rome, people who refused to take responsibility blamed their misfortunes on the stars.

Cassius, a nobleman in Shakespeare's *Julius Caesar*, sets out to challenge this orthodoxy. This is what he says to his friend Brutus: '*The fault*, dear Brutus, is not in *our stars* / But in ourselves, that we are underlings.'

He is basically saying people must begin taking responsibility. They cannot continue blaming fate, or the stars, for the mess they might find themselves in.

In the black community when we are not successful, we, like those ancient Romans, refuse to take responsibility. It is easier and more convenient to blame others.

We refuse to accept that we have possibly failed to apply ourselves in our studies; we refuse to accept that we have failed to throw everything we have into the job at hand.

The easiest escape is to resort to a dark and unfortunate vestige of our belief – witchcraft.

But I digress. To go back to the story of the man from Nelspruit: realising that the situation was fast getting out of hand, the man who was being accused of putting down his brothers and their families convened a family meeting as was his right as a senior brother.

At the meeting he set out the strategy: those of his brothers' children who wanted to go to school and university could rely on him for financial support.

Later, addressing his own wife and children, he explained, 'If they don't go to school, they will continue to be a nuisance to everyone. Even after I am long gone, attacks on you will not relent. So, it is better I bear the cross now, while I am still alive. I will send them to school, thus minimising the damage and possible animosity between you and them in the future. Through education, I will instil independence and a sense of responsibility. If I dismiss them now, I will be creating a climate for an insidious dependency syndrome in the family.'

Two generations later, there are numerous graduates in that extended family. The black tax ploughed back then has borne dividends. It was a major social intervention that turned the fortunes of one extended family.

The permutation of our indebtedness to our immediate family differs from case to case – but it is there. If you don't have siblings who need to be put through school, then you have to pay the loan that your parents had to take out to put you through school. Or you have to repay the aunt or uncle who contributed towards your varsity education.

That's black tax, unique to us. Admittedly, it can be very frustrating for a person who has just started working and is trying to set a foundation for himself to know that the measly salary he will get at the end of the month will have to be divided and sub-divided again. Just so that there is bread on his aunt's table; or that his cousin gets back to school.

Such a person can feel stuck in a vicious cycle of poverty that will never end, unless he wins the lottery. Poverty generally stems from a lack of education. And a lack of education in the black community is the legacy we got from apartheid. It is a sad harvest of thorns.

When the masters of apartheid implemented their strategy of giving black people just enough education to be useful servants, they believed they were being smart. Their immediate aim was to crush creativity and entrepreneurship in the black community. That would create a dependency syndrome. Many black people could not think beyond the next wage envelope, which they could not obtain anywhere else but from a white person.

Sadly, today we are paying a heavy price for the myopia of the apartheid oligarchs who created apartheid and Bantu Education. The Verwoerds and Malans of this world are long gone. The fetid stench of their handiwork, though, is killing the country.

Many in the black majority, though they might have an education, such as it is, are not employable. This is because they do not possess the skills that our modern world demands in order for it to work at its optimum.

Given these economic realities, what is known as black tax will be around for some time still. Those who are able to help should continue helping so the younger generation can go and obtain a meaningful education that will gradually turn things around.

Because of our history, the need to help those who come after us is more discernible in the black community.

Thanks to white privilege, many white people had access to better education. Education does not limit itself to academic exercises inside a classroom. It goes beyond that. It informs how people plan their families. As a result, white people – not because they are intrinsically intelligent, but simply because they were conscientised to family planning at an earlier age – are likely to have smaller families which they can manage.

The smaller the family, the less the financial burden. A no-brainer.

I'm not saying, however, that all white people are trust fund babies born with silver spoons in their mouths. I know some white guys who, upon finishing varsity, have to pay off their study loans, but that's it. They don't have to fix their parents' shack, install electricity at home, pay off their parents' medical bills – or, indeed, pay back some neighbours who would have contributed towards their university education.

No one is celebrating or embracing this black tax. It is, to be honest, an albatross. But if you look at it from a positive angle, it is part of our growth as the black South African community.

When Afrikaners were emerging from English oppression, they experienced something of this sort, where financial obligations had to be shared between parents and their children. To turn things around, the Afrikaners started cooperatives and building societies to stabilise families and build the community, one brick at a time. These micro-ventures, in turn, later grew into formidable entities such as the Saambous, Santams, Sanlams and Naspers of this world.

I am happy that, with each generation, the shackles of black tax are gradually falling off our figurative wrists – as they should. Naturally, it will not happen overnight. We are up against a sad but mammoth legacy of colonial domination and apartheid's economic exploitation.

It's a bitter legacy that goes back four hundred years, when the white hordes – armed with their guns and cannons to kill us, and the Bible to fool and pacify us – descended on the southern tip of this continent and started pushing people off their land, exploiting them, reducing them into beggars and serfs in the land of their forefathers.

FRED KHUMALO is a journalist, essayist, novelist and the author of seven books, both fiction and non-fiction, including *Dancing the Death Drill*. He holds an MA in creative writing from Wits University and is, among other things, a Nieman Fellow at Harvard University and a fellow of the Stellenbosch Institute for Advanced Study. He is currently a PhD candidate at the University of Pretoria.

Welcome to a home everyone calls home . . .

Lucas Ledwaba

What do you do when a complete stranger turns up on your doorstep, asking for a place to stay while he looks for work? Or when a distant relative asks you to take in a truant son who had dropped out of school and was hanging around with the wrong crowd?

Do you flatly turn them down on the grounds that you have seven children to raise and that your home is only a three-bedroomed house with just enough space for your family? Or do you try to explain that you are under a lot of strain as you are in the process of building up your business and money is really tight?

Well, not in the Ledwaba household of the 1980s and early 1990s. At one stage there were as many as 20 people: cousins, children of acquaintances of our parents, great-aunts, uncles and aunts, as well as a few strangers, living with us in our home in Soshanguve.

This was part of the price my parents paid for being among the few in our family who had broken away from their rural roots and set up home in a township. The laws of apartheid condemned those living in rural areas to a life where they were far removed from tertiary institutions and job opportunities.

So, by virtue of us living in a township, our house became a transit station of sorts, a refuge for those in search of economic opportunities or an education.

It also served as a rehabilitation centre of sorts, for relatives who had gone off the rails. Some had fallen victim to the system, in that they found themselves idle in the villages after completing high school because they couldn't find work. Some fell in with the wrong crowd, because their parents did not have the means to enrol them in institutions of higher learning.

Since my parents lived in a township and had their own business, this gave the impression that they were well off and more capable of carrying and feeding extra mouths. Of course, this was far from the truth.

My parents faced struggles of their own and they had to run the rat race like any other parents. Still, they were products of their own beliefs. Their approach was that you never turned away a visitor or a person in need, lest one day you turn away a messenger of God bringing blessings. And so, we got used to strangers randomly walking into our lives, becoming part of our household and family, living rent-free and being supported by our parents.

Because many of those who ended up in our home were older than us children, this meant we often lost the privilege of sleeping in our beds and instead slept on foam mattresses on the floor. We shared everything and there was no special treatment for us. Rather, at times, it seemed as if our parents were more concerned about those they had taken in than their own flesh and blood. It was not uncommon for one to be ordered to give away an item of clothing or even a plate of food.

At mealtimes, the table in our kitchen and the wall cabinets would be packed full of dishes. A stranger who didn't live with us would have been forgiven for thinking we were hosting a gathering when that was in fact our daily reality.

I must say, though, that we didn't see anything wrong with our situation. We were happy and became accustomed to this kind of life, even if our neighbours always found it an intriguing arrangement. To us, used to at least 15 people in the house at any given time, it felt strange to have only three or four people at home. More appeared so much merrier.

In the process several special memories were made and we also learnt valuable life lessons. We learnt the true meaning of the phrase 'sharing is caring': humility and loving without judging people based on their social status or background.

Of course, there was a downside to this set-up. Looking back today, I realise we never really spent quality time with our parents and didn't always get enough attention. Even an outing to a football match or the zoo was often not about us children and our parents alone, since there were always other people in tow.

My poor sisters spent most of their youth cooking and cleaning for the household. In between school and growing up, they were doing more work than most domestic workers could handle. I guess this is the price that is paid by many families, like mine, that opened their hearts and doors to those coming to areas near the city in search of a better life.

I doubt that white families at the time ever had such challenges because the laws of the land had forced black people to become third-class citizens in their own country. They were restricted in every imaginable way. Their freedom of movement was curbed and tightly controlled. They could not live where they wished. They could not study wherever it was most convenient. They were forced by law to live in areas deprived of many essential amenities.

Relatives would travel by bus from far-flung areas and stay over in our home just so they could visit a doctor or sort out personal business. This was long before the era of cellphones, so visitors would show up unannounced. Sometimes, this meant that instead of two chicken feet with your pap,you only had one; or just pap with gravy, while the chicken feet went to the unannounced visitor.

Grumbling about such matters was simply an invitation to trouble; either a tongue lashing from both parents, or worse, an encounter with my father's feared brown belt. Like gold, visitors were treasured and treated with the greatest love and care.

Despite the negative side to this kind of black tax, I'm proud of my parents for the sacrifices they made. They were simple people who recognised the individual's obligation to serve humankind even when circumstances are difficult.

Some of the people they helped went on to make something of their lives. Many became professionals and responsible adults. Yes, some may have fallen along the way, but to this day, they still recognise our parents for giving them an opportunity to become better people.

The open-door policy exposed us to all sorts of colourful characters; like the great aunt who always grumbled and complained of a sore back whenever she saw new visitors. It was a way of ensuring she kept her single bed and was not relegated to the floor as was customary.

Then there was the cousin who always appeared to fake a fit whenever she was in some sort of trouble, and another from the rural areas who had the habit of applying roll-on deodorant to his jacket in the mistaken belief that it was perfume.

One of the strangest encounters happened sometime around 1986, when a stranger showed up on our doorstep. He told the elders his name was David Dlamini and that he had come all the way from Swaziland to look for work in Pretoria. He didn't know a living soul in South Africa and was looking for a place to stay.

For some reason I have yet to understand, in a township with more than 10 000 households, he chose us, the Ledwaba family. Our house was not along the main road, on a street corner or even near a bus terminus, taxi rank or station. Still, this man chose to knock on our door.

Our parents accepted him into their home. There was not even an attempt to verify if this David Dlamini was indeed David Dlamini as he alleged. He could have been Moses Masuku or Patrick Gamedze, for all we knew. Perhaps he was Bafana Dlamini or Jabu Zikalala, even. But that's how it was in our home.

Dlamini, whom we children called the Mswati behind his back, became part of the family. We mimicked the manner in which he spoke and snored as he slept on a foam mattress on the floor of our crowded bedroom.

Not long after he came to live with us, Mswati got a job at the Fresh Produce Market in Pretoria. He often brought home fresh bananas and other fruit. He didn't stay there long, though, because he found another job working for some mlungu in town. One day he came home in a rather chaotic state, barefoot with torn clothes. His boss had beaten him up. And had fired him. But he just laughed it off.

Mswati disappeared from our life just as quickly as he had become a part of it. One day, he announced that he had found a place to stay in Winterveldt. My parents gave him blankets and other things required to start a new home. We never saw him again. After all these years I am still curious about why Mswati picked us.

I can't stop wondering if he was perhaps sent by the gods. I don't know. But he wasn't the first or last to pass through our home.

One day when my brother and I came home for the school lunch break, we found a light-skinned, bearded gentleman seated on a sofa in the lounge, with a pile of bags next to him. After exchanging greetings, he immediately asked for tea, which we served.

That evening we learnt that he would also stay with us. He was the nephew of a man my father had met at a football match some years before – they were both ardent Moroka Swallows fans. And so, when this fellow Swallows fan told my father his nephew was coming to study at the technikon in Soshanguve and had no money to pay for lodgings, my parents took him in without hesitation. He, too, became a part of the family for a good year.

By then my parents had already converted part of the garage into a bedroom where I slept with my cousins and other male occupants of the house. We made many good memories and lasting bonds in that little garage.

If the people who passed through our house during that decade and a half when our parents were still alive had all signed their names on the walls of our house, there would be very little space left. Today I can only thank the gods for giving us parents who never shied away from confronting this so-called black tax.

LUCAS LEDWABA is the editor of Mukurukuru Media. He is also the author of *Broke & Broken: The Shameful Legacy of Gold Mining in South Africa* and a co-author of *We are Going to Kill Each Other Today: The Marikana Story*. He is a journalist and photographer whose work has been published widely in South Africa and abroad.

PART 2

Ungalibali ke, mntanam

Thanduxolo Jika

One day, in 2000, while I was making tea for my parents, I overheard them talking in the lounge. My father was telling my mother that the motor mechanic business he had been working at for many years was shutting down.

This is it, I told myself, now there is no way I am going to walk through the doors of any tertiary institution. At the time I was an A student at Ndzondelelo High School in Zwide, Port Elizabeth, and months away from completing my matric. In an instant my dream of tasting freedom by going to university was in tatters.

But over the next few weeks my mother, a government employee, came to my rescue. A humble clerk, she would sacrifice everything for me and my two siblings to get a tertiary education. Luckily the National Student Financial Aid Scheme (NSFAS) also played a major role and paid for my tuition and residence at Rhodes University in Grahamstown.

(In between getting us educated, my mother also furthered her own studies and got an honours degree. I still do not know how she managed it.)

So, I became the first person in my family to get a tertiary education. This was only possible through a lot of financial sacrifices. Of course, not everything was covered by the bursary and my mother had to take loans to get me through the four years I spent studying.

I recall how excited my parents were when I told them that I would be graduating with a Bachelor of Journalism degree after four years of crawling towards passing my majors, politics and journalism. I had to hire a gown and buy a black suit since I didn't own one. Graduation day, in 2005, was one of their proudest moments. As I walked onto the stage, I could hear my mother ululating from the gallery. It was a teary moment for us all.

I only got to know about the role other people had played when I started working and my mother would ask me to help certain individuals because they had contributed something towards my education and she needed to return the favour. There would be calls from the other relatives I grew up with and the aunts who looked after me when I was young – they had all helped during my time at university.

From 2006, when I found permanent employment, I would always get a friendly reminder from my mother at the end of the month. 'Ungalibali ke, mntanam; don't forget, my child,' are her kind words that tell me there is something I have to settle back home.

I could never forget where I come from. For this reason, I shared the little pay I earned as a junior journalist with my family and paid some of the bills, also during the years my younger siblings went to university. Even when I was later living on my own, I also budgeted for the house in Port Elizabeth. I could not allow the electricity or water to be cut off because my family was under too much financial pressure.

But this is not really how the story starts.

The true origins of how I became one of many young black South Africans who are faced with black tax start on a farm in the Free State. The fact of the matter is that I was born into a family of farm labourers who once were farmers themselves but were kicked off their land due to evil apartheid laws.

When I was born in 1982, my grandparents were working on a farm about 20 kilometres from a small dorpie called Reddersburg, near Bloemfontein in the Free State. My grandparents had six children, four daughters and two sons, one of whom is my father.

At the time, my father was living in Port Elizabeth, because he had been sent there by my grandfather to try and create a better life for himself and escape being a farmworker. My grandfather always said that he despised the working conditions on the farms and that education should be his children's freedom.

My father met my mother in Port Elizabeth. When I was born, they decided to send me to my grandparents, because they couldn't afford a house and were renting. And this is how I came to grow up on the farm with my two aunts, my uncle, my younger brother and our cousin.

I had some of the best times of my life on the farm. Life was all about hunting and swimming in the nearby rivers, with nothing to worry about. We looked after cattle, sheep and goats and hunted all kinds of animals; that's where I fell in love with rabbit and porcupine meat..

The worst thing, though, was when the damned goats would go missing and we would have to look for them with my uncle and cousin. This meant long walks in the mountains, and confrontations with snakes and other dangerous animals. Fortunately, I had faith in and trusted our most ferocious hunting dogs, Tiger and Blackie.

I remember the day, in 1988, when a magical thing happened and our beautiful life was interrupted. It was shortly after Christmas. I remember this because my parents had visited us on the farm and had bought me new clothes for Christmas, as well as takkies. If I remember correctly, they were North Stars. They had also brought us a television set.

It was the first time I had seen a television, powered by a generator. I vividly remember those first black and white images, a music video of what I later came to know as one of the most popular South African music groups, Bayete. It was a video of the song 'Mbombela'.

It was also the first time I had seen a train, as it was shown on the video. The video was followed by another where men were riding horses. I could relate to it because I had tried riding my grandfather's horse but fell. I was to learn later that the men in the video were part of Sankomota, another powerful music group.

This was the happiest day of my life because I saw another world in the television set, even though the picture was not perfect despite my father's numerous instructions to my uncle – on the roof – to move the aerial to different places. I didn't care how blurry the picture was (I knew no better) and neither did my grandfather, as he continually asked my father excitedly, 'Yintoni lento? What is this thing?'

At the time, I thought the people we were seeing on television lived inside the box. However, after that day I don't recall the television ever being switched on again, I can only assume because my grandparents could not afford petrol for the generator.

But one morning, my beautiful life, with no worries about anything, changed. I was woken up at the same time as my uncle and cousin, the time they usually got up to go to school. It was still dark, around five o'clock in the morning, and they prepared the fire and water in the big, black, three-legged pot for bathing. There was no electricity, bathtub or hot shower; we bathed in a 'waskom' – indishi.

I remember the long walk to our school, Beang tse Molemo Combined School, on the N6 to Reddersburg. The distance to school and back amounted to about 40 kilometres a day and we were to walk it for at least a year, until my grandfather sold his livestock, quit as a farmworker and bought a house in Reddersburg.

From then on, until I was a teenager, I grew up in Reddersburg. We survived on my grandparents' government pensions because no farmworker ever gets a pay-out from his or her employers, or even Unemployment Insurance Fund (UIF) benefits. My grandfather did the odd garden job in the white areas and that fed a family that by now consisted of over eight people.

When I was in Standard 3 or 4 (Grade 5 or 6) my school shoes were completely worn out. This, despite the fact that for over a year my grandfather had done his best to fix them. I then had to go and make a call from the public phone to my mother, who was a clerk at the Department of Education, to ask for money for new school shoes. She agreed and I don't know how the money was sent to my grandparents, but they bought me a pair of Idlers.

By then, my aunt had dropped out of school and had her

own children. At some point my grandfather could not afford to look after all of us any longer and asked my parents to take us to Port Elizabeth. As teenagers, my brother and I were sent to Port Elizabeth to live with my parents and our younger sister. We arrived to what is these days described as a middle-class life; my parents had bought a house and were both working. That is, until the year when my father lost his job.

When my grandfather passed away in 2009, three years after I had started working, I did not forget what I had to do. I am the eldest son and I knew what my father's expectation of me would be.

A giant had fallen, a wise man who had raised us with his meagre farmworker's wage and, later, his pension. He deserved a proper burial. When my father made the call to me, I did not hesitate – I took a train from East London, where I was based at the time, back to Reddersburg. Even though I myself didn't have much, I realised that I was more privileged than everyone else in the family. I simply had to help out back home.

The reality is that helping out in this way becomes more difficult with the escalating costs of living, establishing your own family, looking after your own property and getting a vehicle. There is a misunderstanding by certain family members that since I appear on television now and again, I must have a lot of money. If there is a need for an imicimbi, a family gathering, there is a natural expectation that I will assist in making sure it happens, by chipping in more than everyone else.

Many of us have black tax on our backs, but this is a responsibility we cannot walk away from. What is important is to never forget the history behind us and the class we were born into and what we have already achieved. Ungalibali ke, mntanam.

THANDUXOLO JIKA is a co-author of *We are Going to Kill Each Other Today: The Marikana Story* and a multi-award-winning investigative journalist who is now the *Mail & Guardian* newspaper's Investigations Editor. He has tackled major investigations of national importance, from telling of the xenophobic killings of Somali nationals in the townships of East London, to bringing to South Africans the faces of Marikana victims who were massacred by police in 2012 and exposing state capture by the Guptas and their associates.

An ode to Mme Mpoleleng Sebatla, a grandmother

Lucas Moloi

When night falls, a group of young and old women from White City, Jabavu, in Soweto, hit the streets carrying huge buckets and bowls full of cooked cow trotters and sheep heads. When they reach the corner of Phera and Mlangeni Streets, they place their merchandise on the sidewalk in an orderly manner to sell to their customers.

The women have a cordial relationship with each other, but there is law and order here – every seller knows exactly where her spot is. Should anyone want to join these women in business, she has to be formally introduced to the others and allocated a spot. But her application is likely to be turned down, especially when the business of selling cow trotters and sheep heads is not doing so well. The smaller the group, the fatter the slice of the pie each woman will take home to her family.

Motorists had better park carefully when they buy from these women. Some will shout profanities at a driver when they feel he is obscuring them from other potential buyers.

Among these women is the 69-year-old Mme Mpoleleng Sebatla, from the mountain kingdom of Lesotho. In 1989, acute poverty and unemployment in her country forced her to leave her home. She went to look for a job in Johannesburg in order to be able to support herself and send money back home. She worked as a domestic worker for several years until rheumatism weakened her body.

Despite her deteriorating health, going back to poverty-stricken Lesotho was not an option. She had just lost her daughter to illness and she had to take care of her granddaughter, Nthabeleng. Like many other young Basotho ladies, Mme Mpoleleng's daughter had also left Lesotho, with a baby on her back, in search of a better life, leaving the child's father behind, possibly because he could not take care of them. Had life been easier at home, she surely would not have risked going to the dog-eat-dog city of Johannesburg.

Mme Mpoleleng had to beat the odds and her rheumatism to feed and provide for her granddaughter. Instead of nursing herself back to health, she rented a shack in Soweto and joined other Basotho nationals who sold sheep heads and cow trotters. It was a daunting task, often done in terrible weather conditions, but she had to do it. They were in a foreign country without any relatives. For Nthabeleng, her grandmother was her only beacon of hope.

Today, Nthabeleng is like any 16-year-old child who is well taken care of. She is a learner at the iconic Morris Isaacson Secondary School in White City, one of the schools that was at the forefront of the 1976 student uprising. On that fateful day, learners in Soweto were protesting against the use of Afrikaans as a medium of instruction, when they were shot at by the police.

Usually, young people who have just started a new job help to renovate or build houses for their families and support them in other ways after they have found employment. Of course, some families are bigger, while other families have unemployed uncles and aunties and their children, who live in rooms or even shacks in backyards and also need to be taken care of. Many people call this phenomenon 'black tax'.

It's often the learned youngsters, who think these gestures are holding them back from living their dreams, who use the term 'black tax' with silent disdain. Perhaps Mme Mpoleleng is not that 'educated', but for her, looking after Nthabeleng is simply her familial responsibility.

'I am thankful that I sell magcina. We don't roam the streets naked. I just bought my grandchild a school uniform worth R2 500. I can afford to buy her some of the basics that children her age need,' Mme Mpoleleng says.

Even though she is older than 60, she doesn't have a South African identity document and therefore does not qualify for the state's monthly pension grant of R1 690 and neither does Nthabeleng qualify for the child support grant of R410.

'I did not want to beg for handouts at street corners,' she says proudly. 'I rolled up my sleeves and I started to work.'

Mme Mpoleleng's day usually starts around 05:00. 'If you sleep, you'll eat the excrement of other women,' she says loosely. Or put differently: you snooze, you lose.

At dawn, she is already queuing for trotters at a depot not far from Chris Hani Baragwanath Hospital, in Diepkloof. Competition is tight as she is not the only one who sells this delicacy. People travel long distances to arrive before the depot opens.

'You won't find anything to sell if you get here late. What would we eat, should I not sell anything for the day?' she asks, not expecting an answer from anyone but herself. 'It would be a day wasted.'

She must arrive early at the depot because she buys sheep heads elsewhere and must catch another taxi to reach her next destination.

Mme Mpoleleng rents a tiny one-room shack in one of the yards in White City. Her sanctuary is among four others that are squeezed into the yard. The landlord's two-room brick house stands in the middle. There's scarcely enough space in the yard to move around without bumping into one another or turning sideways to make way for another person.

This shack is what Mme Mpoleleng and Nthabeleng call home. Everything they own is stored in the room: a grocery store trolley she uses to carry her stock, bags of clothes, plastic tubs for bathing, a shelf and other paraphernalia. Grandmother and granddaughter share a double bed.

'Sometimes when I want to sleep more restfully, I kick my grandchild out of the bed. She sleeps on the floor,' she says jokingly.

On the day I visit her, the temperature in Soweto exceeds 30°C; inside the shack, you would swear the mercury has gone above 40°C. It is exacerbated by the small space, corrugated iron walls and a two-plate stove that is heating up a large, simmering pot, full of trotters. The stove contests for space with some utensils, shoes and bags of groceries that could not be packed on the worn-out shelf.

'It is hard work,' Mme Mpoleleng says with sweat streaming down her face. 'We have to shave these heads clean before we cook them. They take about two hours to be well-cooked. Cow feet take more than three hours,' she says. She has to burn the bristles on the trotters, then scrubs off the soot until they are clean, smooth and ready to be cooked. It requires great effort and patience.

Sometimes, business takes a dive due to a few bad apples amongst the group of women.

'Those without refrigerators sell expired and nasty smelling meat. As a result, the customers think all of us sell bad food and then they end up buying elsewhere,' one of the ladies complains to me.

A half-skop – a sheep head cut in half – costs about thirty rands. A full cow trotter sells for the same price. Alternatively, she cuts the hoof into three pieces and sells each for R10. In addition to the half-skop and trotters, she sells dumplings.

Mme Mpoleleng's business hours start at seven o'clock in the evening and she toils until the early hours of the following day. Her customers are clubbers and partygoers who leave their entertainment venues in the early hours of the morning.

'I love them with passion. They are the reason we stay up until the morning. They support our business,' she says. 'Our only distractors are the Metro Police. I have lost five bowls to them. Every time we see them, we hurriedly pack our items and run. But we have children to look after, hence we come back.'

On a bad day, she takes home R300 and when she's lucky, she earns about R600. But even the bad days and the pestering by Metro Police officers don't deter her, nor does extreme weather, nor the treacherous streets she has to brave to and from her selling point. From her meagre income, she looks after herself and Nthabeleng and saves for a rainy day.

Mme Mpoleleng's legs are slowly giving in. They are swollen and she's forced to walk around barefoot, grimacing from the pain. Rheumatism is taking its toll and they can no longer carry her like they used to.

'If it all fails, I will take my belongings and go back to Lesotho. I have no relatives here. When I die, I want to be laid to rest among my people back home,' she says.

But she hopes that when the end comes, Nthabeleng will at least have received a good education and will be able to sustain herself – and continue the tradition of helping those who come after her.

LUCAS MOLOI hails from Itsoseng township, in the North West province. He is a BTech Journalism graduate from the Tshwane University of Technology. Moloi worked as a journalist for Kaya FM and is currently a television current affairs news producer for the South African Broadcasting Corporation. He has also worked on films like *Hotel Rwanda* and written a few scripts for a vernacular sitcom, *Ga Re Dumele.*

The power of black tax

Nokubonga Mkhize

Thousands of South Africans are responsible for looking after two generations – not only their children but their parents, too. Some call them the sandwich generation, but I just call it living with black tax. I am where I am today thanks to black tax and the story of my family shows the power of black tax.

My grandmother left the homelands at Umkomaas at the tender age of 19. It was soon after the death of her husband, uMkhulu. She was married at 16 years old. In my culture, isiZulu, women are traditionally trained for marriage, while young men are trained to provide for their families.

But boy, oh boy, did the game change when our wealth – land – was taken away from us: uGogo akasakwazi ukulima, she could no longer work the soil for food, and so she had to head to the city to earn money.

For the time being Gogo had to leave her only daughter, Thandi, in the rural areas with her sisters. They might not have called it black tax, but they didn't think twice about helping their sister.

After months of searching, she eventually found a job in the warm home of an old German couple in Durban. After working for a few months, Gogo was finally able to bring her daughter – my mother – to the city. My mother often tells funny stories about this time. Once, she ate dog food thinking it was mincemeat with bones, and then there was her daily encounter with oats. According to my grandmother, oats porridge was the reason white kids were so intelligent. She would therefore force-feed my mother oats because she wanted her to be the best at school. My mother hated it; all she wanted was ordinary maize porridge.

Gogo desired a lavish lifestyle and therefore she wanted her kids to do well so that they could one day own properties like her employer's. As a domestic worker, she thought there was no hope for her anyway.

A few years later, when my mother was old enough to look after herself, she moved to a place called Clermont, just outside Pinetown. She lived in a squatter camp called Kwashembe, since it was closer to her school. Of course, during apartheid, black kids were not allowed to attend white schools.

Kwashembe had no electricity or even running water. Your bedroom was your kitchen, which was also turned into a bathroom every morning. Living conditions were worse than at Umkomaas because back home there was at least enough room.

Fortunately, the people who lived there were very helpful and generally very protective. My mother soon became part of the community. She also became good friends with ugogo uMgoma, a friend of my grandmother's and a sangoma, who then became her second mother; a guardian angel in the fast-paced city.

Then 1976 happened.

The Soweto uprising, or should we call it the youth uprising? It led to so much chaos in the townships that there was actually no hope of education. My mother also toyi-toyied in the streets of Clermont with the other students.

Gogo had absolutely no idea that my mother was suddenly a freedom fighter. She did not want anything to do with politics, because to her it only represented an easy way to lose your life. I guess this is where Gogo's dream of living in a luxurious home as big as white people's homes ended. Apartheid had deprived her only child of an education.

After months of suspended classes my mother had to join a cotton firm, working shifts from six to six. Soon, she had kids of her own, including me and my older brother Themba, and as her family grew, it became even harder for her to go back to school.

I remember how Themba used to babysit me; he was already in high school then. He was the boy with a baby stroller at soccer practice, but he did not mind because he understood that mommy had to go to work. Themba was so good at soccer that the coach would never let him miss a game. If Themba had to babysit, the coach would fetch us and would hold me throughout the 90 minutes of the game. If you ask me, that was another form of black tax.

One thing my mother never compromised on was education. When I was just seven, I had to go to boarding school because Themba had to start university and there was no one to look after me when my mother had to work double shifts.

One afternoon, after spending all day registering on campus, Themba came home with news that would eventually change our family's economic status for good.

'Ma! Ma!' he cried, as he ran into the house with a few papers in his hands. 'Ma, I got NSFAS!' he shouted.

At that moment my mother did not even know that he was talking about the National Student Financial Aid Scheme. Themba beamed with excitement.

'Ma, this means you don't have to worry about my university fees anymore, the government will loan me money to study.'

My mother breathed a sigh of relief, 'So, I don't have to worry about all those thousands of rands anymore? Jehova umkhulu!'

The following year, I started my primary school journey at boarding school and a few years later I completed my matric. At that point, I had big dreams about becoming the next Oprah Winfrey. I wanted to study for a Bachelor of Social Science in Communications at the University of Pretoria, but Themba wasn't happy.

'I do not want you to go to the University of Pretoria, Nokubonga,' he told me one day, looking grave and concerned. 'Who will look after you? How will I get to you when you are sick? If you live in the same province, at least I can always send you food.'

'But it is my dream, it is the only place my career can survive,' I mumbled under my breath, upset and angry as a bull.

'I don't care, Nokubonga, I don't have that kind of money,' Themba said.

It was the most difficult conversation I have ever had with my brother. I was stuck between my dreams and the reality of our finances. There was nothing left to do but to suck it up and register at a local university.

I was part of Themba's budget for the entire duration of my university life. When I look back now, I am not sure how we all survived on his intern's salary of just R3 500. This R3 500 ensured that I had food every month and, darling, my hair was always on point. I often heard stories from my classmates about how they had to eat Kellogg's for dinner. Maybe I was not much of a big eater, but I always had food and mostly also meat.

As a student, I also had a number of socials to attend. I was not really a party animal, but I loved clothes. So, a portion of my allowance would be put aside to buy clothes. I'm quite sure, today, that the money Themba gave me could've been enough for a car instalment.

My mother has also always been paying black tax. She housed relatives who sought employment or were looking to study in the city. All these people became aunts and uncles, and even today we still assist their kids. You can just begin to imagine how far black tax reaches, but this is our culture.

Some of the relatives who stayed with us would contribute, others would not or could not. My brother's payments helped to support them, too.

I remember one guy who was the son of a one of my mom's friends. He would avoid dinner every night because he did not want to contribute towards the groceries. When his girlfriend came over, he would buy KFC for just the two of them and they would lock themselves in his room. He never even considered the electricity and water he used.

But then there was someone like Sonto, who had moved to the city to find a teaching job. She would give my mom a portion of her salary for groceries. This made it easier for my brother to focus on me and my studies.

My mom never expected any rent – those who were working

simply had to contribute what they could. And if someone decided that they could not or would not contribute, no questions were asked.

A very frustrating part of black tax is the expectations parents have of their children. They simply assume that once you have been to university you will receive a decent pay cheque. Regardless of your chosen profession or whether you're still doing an internship, they believe you are earning as much as a doctor. For the mere fact that you have completed a three-year degree, you are richer than Mam' Dolly's daughter who did not go to university.

It is even worse if you work in a different city, Johannesburg to be specific. It does not matter if you live in the slums of the CBD; according to the folks back home, you are living a life of luxury. When I was working in Johannesburg in 2013, I had an aunt who used to call me for imali ye drink – 'money for cool drink'. However, this cool drink money was not your normal R20 for a two-litre. No, this was a 'You work in Joburg and I deserve to get at least R200' demand. If I dared to say I did not have money, she would tell the rest of the family what a stingy child I was.

I was probably better off than most, though. One of my friends had a brother who was obsessed with Carvelas. These shoes cost more than R1 000 a pair, but her brother, who was still in high school, insisted on the brand. And it wasn't even as if these Carvelas motivated him to get good marks.

The reality of black tax really hit me when I started working. I realised then, that when we're young, we take so many things for granted. Many youngsters have an I-deserve-to-be-taken-care-of attitude and don't know where money comes from and what it takes to give up a portion of your salary to an ungrateful person. Not that I wasn't grateful, but maybe I just didn't feel it that deep, hey?

I saw another side to things when I was briefly married to a man who never really understood black tax. I remember crying so hard just to be allowed to give my mother R500. And I mean, what can you even do with a mere R500? The worst part was that it was my salary, my hard-earned cash, but I had said okwami owakho, what's mine is yours.

Then it was that argument of well, if you give your mother money, we must give my parents money, too. But I don't remember him even budgeting for this. I thought to myself, *But both your parents work; why is this even a factor?*

Month end would be horrible. I would visit home with a few plastic bags, knowing very well that my mother needed more. I even began to avoid going home and just sent the R500.

This time in my life made me understand the frustration my brother felt when I told him I was getting married while I was still a student. I was already engaged by my graduation day. The fact that I could not honour my one and only parent was probably one of the contributing factors to the marriage falling apart. To me, my husband's actions translated as a form of hatred. Hatred for my family and a disregard for what was important to me.

Today, it is so wonderful to be able to take care of everything at home. Although, I must say, it can get a little frustrating at times. It mostly has to do with my 42-year-old brother, Jomo, who still lives with us and yes, he is our responsibility. Now, Jomo is the hood rat king, in fact, he is beyond being a hood rat. He's like a living ancestor looking over all of us but never committing to a job.

Jomo is generally sweet to our relatives and when we have imcimbi or a funeral at home, he is usually the go-to guy for almost everything. Jomo can cook all three cows on his own but can't keep a job for more than three months.

He has a best friend and this friend's name is ingudu. This beer is bought with the money he steals from us. He once admitted that while he does not like stealing, otikoloshe direct him and tell him where we hide our cash. I have since learnt not to keep cash on hand, but it is very hard since I use public transport.

However, I was really proud of him when he dedicated himself to a cleaning job in one of the hotels in town. But when that contract ended, he was back to his old self and turned into a toll gate again; to get past him, you would have to fork out some money.

What is really annoying is that when he manages to get a piece job nyana, he goes jolling. He drinks from Sunday to Monday and comes back to eat the food *we* buy. If it was not for my mother, I am sure I would be starving him by now, but Themba always says, 'Ngeke simlahle,' we can never discard him.

Usually, when you look after someone, the expectation is that they would do the same for you. Jomo is not that person, he wouldn't even paint Themba's house for free. He wanted a pair of sneakers in return! Themba understands his mentality. Maybe I do, too, but I won't accept it. I will never accept someone having no vision or aspirations for his own life.

Do I feel frustrated at times? Of course. I'm a 27-year-old with no car and no property. Between dealing with a jobless South Africa and black tax, hell, I'm very frustrated.

I work in a company where I am the only one without a car. Now, you know those embarrassing moments, where everybody heads to the car park and you take the opposite route and then you still have to fight with the taxi drivers. Those are my worst! I have also had to say no to lunch hook-ups because I cannot afford it, because I live on a budget.

My gosh, I should be living my life.

And then there are the never-ending baby showers, birthdays and bridal showers where you are expected to – and also want to – contribute, because in black culture we help each other and often the person who has the celebration doesn't have much money. But the type of friends I have will organise a gift registry – don't ever think you can rob them with a baby set from China Mall!

I once had a very embarrassing moment when one of my friends was having her 30th birthday party. I dressed up and went to the fancy restaurant where the party was held. It had such a beautiful view and wow, everything looked so expensive. The prices on the menu did not suit my freelancer's salary, but since I wasn't familiar with this kind of birthday party, I had assumed the meal would be paid for.

At the end of the night the bill arrived. It seemed I was the only one who was not aware that the guests had to pay. I survived that night only because my partner had slipped a few notes into my handbag. Bottom line is, this is the kind of black tax we never discuss, the one that we don't plan for, but must pay for.

My personal story echoes the stories of many of the people I interviewed for my honours thesis about the phenomenon of black tax. I realised that for many families, black tax is this huge elephant in the room that is never addressed because of our cultural background.

When I completed my thesis, I thought that maybe we should redefine black tax. Maybe it should be defined as the money that black professionals contribute to look after their families, who were never able to create wealth or financial stability during the previous regime. As black families we have been disadvantaged when it comes to generational wealth and we cannot run away from this fact.

The thing is, many people, regardless of their race or background, support their families, but the difference lies in whether it's a choice. Some choose to help, others *have to*.

As much as black tax is a responsibility for most of the people I interviewed, they don't see it as such a burden. When it does become a problem, it's not the actual finances but the emotional burden. For example, one of the interviewees said, while she doesn't mind paying her brother's school fees, it becomes a burden when he fails because he does not dedicate himself to his studies. Someone else also pointed out that the burden is when you see no improvement; when you buy groceries for your siblings, but they do not appreciate your efforts or even try to look for a job to assist you with paying the bills.

We cannot change the world overnight, but we can start with our families. It might seem like a far-fetched idea that someday our families will be well off, but as long as we have good financial discipline and wealth goals, it is possible to achieve. I know I might sound like a motivational speaker now, promising miracles, but I once read that six months of financial focus can give you five years of good returns, which, to me, means financial stability.

There is also some satisfaction in knowing exactly where your money is going. I also feel lucky that thanks to black tax, I have not accumulated debt.

Our black tax commitments might be difficult at times, but at least we are never alone in it. What keeps us going are those grateful smiles, every time we walk in at the end of the month carrying plastic bags filled with Ultramel and NikNaks.

NOKUBONGA MKHIZE, also known as 'Bonga Thezuludiamond', is a corporate media whizz. She holds an honours degree in Media and Cultural Studies from the University of KwaZulu-Natal. Nokubonga is an established voice-over artist for several major media houses and also dabbles as an MC and session broadcaster. She has worked with brands such as BNCommunications, TransAfrica Radio, Inanda FM, Durban Youth TV, Splendid Marketing, Tourism Kwazulu-Natal and Open Africa. Through her company, Azi Diamante, she hopes to establish mentoring programmes for young women in the media industry.

The door at 1842 Mankuroane Street that let black tax in

Outlwile Tsipane

My 88-year-old grandmother must be the greatest social worker who is actually a qualified teacher. Whenever I tell her this, she laughs it off. It becomes a to and fro between us, with her nonchalantly dismissing my praises for her countless selfless deeds over the years.

'What could I have done, ngwana'a ngwanake? Kana mabogo dinku a a thebana,' she would say, instilling in me the lesson that tasks and problems are better tackled and overcome when people come together to help each other.

'This life is tough and it is only God who knows why and we dare not question him.'

I know of her acts of kindness because I am her grandson and I lived under her roof at 1842 Mankuroane Street, in Huhudi, near Vryburg, from birth until Standard 7 (Grade 9), when I changed schools and moved to Bloemfontein. At the hive of activity that was her house, I saw with my own eyes the comings and goings of relatives and the acceptance of strangers into this house. And there have been many other accounts, way before I was born, of people entering the door of her house in need of help.

I was a curious child who often interrogated her. I wanted

to know her story, or perhaps rather her history. At each turn of my commission of inquiry into her life, I was astounded by how she repeatedly committed herself to a specific cause that demanded a lot of sacrifice. Her only remuneration was seeing the happiness of those she had helped.

My grandmother started her teaching career in 1950 after obtaining her qualification from Tiger Kloof Educational Institute, a school 15 kilometres south of Huhudi, that was run by the London Missionary Society. It counts among its alumni two presidents of Botswana, borre Quett Ketumile Masire le Seretse Ian Khama.

By 1952, from her wages of R3 working as a teacher at Barolong Primary School, she had saved enough money to build her parents a brick and cement house in the village of Ganyesa, where she was born. The structure caused quite a sensation because it was the first of its kind. With glee in her eyes, my grandmother would tell me how the people of the village dubbed it 'ntlo ya semente', 'the house of cement'.

Building a house for her family was her way of being thankful, as she puts it, to her father and her sisters, who cared for her after her mother passed away when she was just nine months old. Her father remarried and soon the household burgeoned with siblings from his second marriage. A contribution of groceries – and sometimes a monthly stipend – would follow on the 'house of cement', which now stood so firm and proud.

The quaint structure is still intact today. It has been refurbished, but it is still in its original form and it now serves as a spaza shop that is hired out to Ethiopian shopkeepers.

Of course, it was only natural that my grandmother would

want to have a family of her own. She had gotten married to her beau by the time she built this house and they had one of their own in Huhudi. The first of my mother's four daughters was born in 1957. This daughter would later actually become a social worker, obtaining her degree at Turfloop University (today the University of Limpopo).

Tradition dictates that a woman should be guided through the first steps of motherhood by her own mother or an experienced relative. When her first daughter was born, the role of assisting my grandmother fell to her sister, who, during this period, left her own family back in Johannesburg, where, now married, she was staying with her family in the Main Reef area.

However, the atrocious laws of the apartheid government dealt harshly with black female teachers. They could only get temporary employment and had no maternity leave benefits. Black teachers who fell pregnant, which is essentially a basic human right, simply lost their jobs.

My grandmother relayed to me what a dehumanising effect this had on her. It meant that she had to apply anew in order to return to the profession. This usually had to happen as soon as the baby was over a month or so old, leaving mothers with very little opportunity to bond with them.

My grandmother was now without an income and her husband was struggling to find employment in a small town with limited economic opportunities. But that didn't get her down; she simply marched forth. I have to admire her indomitable spirit and industrious nature.

At that time there were very few schools for black children in the area, which stretched to the west of Vryburg, the deep rural areas of Morokweng and Madibogo, extending to the modern-day Northern Cape towns of Kuruman and Warrenton. When her 'maternity leave' came to an end in the middle of the winter of 1957, my grandmother left my grandfather behind in Vryburg and, with her infant, braved the cold to travel to these remote parts and take on a new teaching post.

In this era, many schools were run on church premises established by missionaries. As the number of learners increased in these mission schools, the church premises proved inadequate. My grandmother became involved in projects to relocate these schools to other buildings. This was done with the lobbying of the community, the education department and also the church.

She tells me all of this with an air of confidence and pride, her eyes wide and glistening behind her thick-framed spectacles. This tenacious vein has become part of her legacy, which is etched into the fibre of more than a dozen schools in the region.

During this time, the assistance of strangers-turned-friends came in handy through offerings of lodgings and other necessities. In between, she had to look after her marriage and in 1961 her second daughter was born, followed by my mother in 1964.

One of my grandmother's sisters was living in Orlando West, in Soweto, just two blocks from the now famous Vilakazi Street precinct where the Mandela and Tutu houses are situated. This would become the place my mother called home as a small child and during her primary schooling. My grandmother had decided to send her to Soweto, as it was tough moving around with three young girls.

'Akere wa tlhaloganya ngwana'a ngwanake? Moving around with your mother and her sisters was proving difficult. My sister helped me, just like all those years ago when they were my pillars from being a toddler to adulthood,' my grandmother tells me.

I nod, showing my understanding of the deeper emotional meaning of these words.

When my mother fell pregnant with me she was still in her matric year. It was quite a disappointment for my grandmother and grandfather, but their displeasure turned into elation when I was born as the first boy in the family. My mother had by now moved back to Huhudi, after my grandmother was finally able to secure a teaching position there. Sadly, in 1984, when I was just nine months old, Grandfather passed away.

By then, Grandmother's teaching career had blossomed – she had been teaching for nearly 30 years and had been appointed principal of Retlaadira Primary School in 1975. She was now a widow with three grandchildren to look after. Although we provided some solace to her, the added responsibility must've been a burden, even though she would never complain about it.

When we became of schoolgoing age, Grandmother made sure we looked immaculate in our school uniforms. After all, she was principal at the school we attended. We never wanted for anything, whether it was food, clothing, games or medical care.

At times I sit and wonder, what could have become of my grandmother? What could she have done for herself had she not sacrificed so much for our family? Would she have travelled the world? Would she have built herself a bigger house or bought a car? How would certain parts of her life have been different had she not made the sacrifices she did? Every little sacrifice for us and others was an opportunity lost to do something for herself.

And we were not the only ones that she touched with her generosity. As time went by, I witnessed more and more acts of sacrifice and kindness at 1842 Mankuroane Street, in Huhudi. Small acts, seemingly insignificant, but telling.

For example, the television she owned was a rare thing and created much traffic from kids in the neighbourhood who would come to watch a popular drama series at eight. In summer, when the high temperatures would take their toll, a neighbour would call and pass a two-litre bottle over the fence to be stored in the fridge. Another might just ask for a glass of ice-cold water. Or on a Monday, there would be someone coming to ask for the newspapers from the past week that my grandmother regularly bought.

Constantly, this or that person was staying with us, either a distant relative or one of their kids, and some even attended school with us. I vividly remember the year 1992. The political climate suggested that there was some kind of change on the horizon. That year we were joined by a distant cousin of ours, whose father was a minister in the former Bophuthatswana government. I was made to understand that things were not so cosy back there and that is why they needed to stay with us before proceeding to a boarding school the following year.

Another memorable event that showed the extent of my grandmother's open-door policy took place in the winter of 1993. That was one of the years of yellow maize as there was a drought. There was a group of Zimbabwean women who had been going around our community selling all kinds of wares, like tablecloths and cushions. My grandmother was their client and would always be very hospitable towards them, serving them tea and scones if we had any.

During one such visit by the Zimbabwean women, they had convinced my grandmother, with little reluctance on her part, I suppose, that they should occupy our backyard dwelling, which served as a storage facility. My grandmother also let them share the kitchen with us.

I learnt a lot from them, from how they cooked to a bit of the chiShona language. Given the predominance of yellow maize at the time, the word sadza, for pap, has stayed with me ever since. I rank this episode as one of the most generous and selfless of my grandmother's gestures.

I also remember, in 1996, being assigned the task of looking after a girl my grandmother had adopted from one of the villages that surrounded Vryburg. Hers was a sensitive story, as her adoptive grandmother had been arrested after human flesh was found in pots in her house. She's now a married woman with her own family, living happily in Bloemfontein.

The effects of the politics of the time were also felt. The apartheid police burned down a relative's house, someone we simply referred to as an uncle. My grandmother stepped in and brought his children to stay with us, whilst their father and mother went into hiding.

That we had a telephone line at 1842 Mankuroane Street was quite a big thing and the source of many memories. I still remember our number – 6183 – before the new ten-digit system was introduced. My grandmother's telephone basically served as a community phone. Families living in our street received calls there, often without my grandmother's consent. Once, there was a knock in the dead of night: it was a man whose daughter was heavily pregnant and needed an ambulance.

Another memorable call – one that I eavesdropped on – came from America. It was from a distant relative who lived there, to whom Granny had sent a few rands. Since this faraway place was only known to me via television, I had all kinds of questions for my grandmother after the call. Instead of chastising me for listening in on an adult conversation, something we children were always being warned against, she shook her head and gave a wry smile before letting me in on the contents of the conversation. I would bet my bottom rand she would have worked in a life lesson of sorts to say, 'people shall share'. This is a phrase she uttered many, many times.

There was a time, when I was growing up, when my father left his job at a platinum mine in a town we know today as Marikana, due to the fighting that flared up between the different ethnic groups working at the mine. It meant that my father and mother came to live under my grandmother's roof. This is something that was considered culturally taboo, but that didn't bother her.

Everything my grandmother did over the years encapsulates what black tax is all about. However, I have misgivings about this term, which I believe is, in essence, a misnomer. Tax is something you have to pay by law, but no law compels you to help your family or strangers.

What some people call black tax is something that has been at the core of our existence, *my* existence. The concept doesn't point to anything new. Rather, it merely describes something that has been happening within black society for many decades and over several generations. We share our financial and other means with our families, often also our extended families.

We must see black tax for what it is and understand how this phenomenon came to be – it is a consequence of the unjust apartheid system. For this reason, it particularly affects us as black people.

At an ideological level, it is something I vehemently oppose, but this is the perspective we need to consider it from, I believe: our children, the future generations, should not have to navigate such challenging conditions and should be able to enjoy the fruits of their labour.

I suppose I picked up many of my personality traits from my grandmother. I find it difficult to say no to people and I am always ready to offer help, even if it ends up being to my detriment. Not that I am anywhere near being as selfless as my grandmother, but in my adult life, I have taken in family or the friend who has just gotten a new job and needs a place to stay for a few months.

In my personal life, I have definitely paid my black tax dues. Inadvertently, we all do.

OUTLWILE TSIPANE is a father of one. He loves books and travelling. When the situation allows, he combines these two favourite pastimes by going to literature festivals and events, both locally and on the rest of the African continent. Together with other book lovers, he has organised events that enhance the culture of reading in faraway places normally starved of such activities. Through these ventures, he sells books, too. His opinion pieces and book reviews have been featured in *The Elephant* in Kenya and locally the *Johannesburg Review of Books*. He is also an entrepreneur and has recently started his own multifaceted property consultancy, after working for ten years in that industry.

PART 3

Keeping our ancestral spirit of ubuntu alive

Niq Mhlongo

How did we allow this ugly term – 'black tax'– to become part of our vocabulary? And by 'we' I mean all the people who, like me, have lived and benefited from this informal system of sharing and helping each other out. I think I might be confused.

All along, I was convinced that giving is a sign of ubuntu, one of the oldest African traditions. To me, helping members of my family is a non-negotiable responsibility – a symbol of the continuity of time and the immortality of the family soul. As Africans, we live a communal life, don't we? At least this is how I was raised at home. Like they say, if a child is made to see beauty, it grows up into the likeness of that beauty. I have always only seen beauty in sharing and helping my family.

Maybe I have become desensitised to what others see as the exploitative nature of 'black tax'? Maybe I need a debriefing, just like everyone else who takes a traditional and spiritual view on this very sensitive topic.

I first heard the term 'black tax' during the economic recession that hit the world in the late 2000s. Before then, there was no such term. If it was called something like this, it must have been mentioned in private spaces only and in whispers, because it would've been seen as inappropriate. In most of the sections of Soweto that I lived in, it was simply 'family duty', 'family plans', 'family responsibility', 'family upliftment' or 'family obligation'.

An expression popularly used in the township at the time, the one that is closest to the concept of 'black tax', is 'toll gates'. This phrase referred to the amount you would spend on the streets when you visited your neighbourhood, even before entering the gates of your family home. It is common to hear someone say, 'I'm not using that street again because there are many toll gates.'

After e-tolls were introduced in Gauteng, people quickly substituted 'toll gate' with 'e-toll'. When you hear them say 'Jabu is an e-toll,' it means you can't pass a particular street without giving someone (Jabu) money. It can be your unemployed friend asking you for R2 to buy a cigarette, your sister's ex-boyfriend who wants you to buy him a quart of beer or a neighbour who has been in jail asking for R10 for the train fare to Johannesburg.

This is an everyday affair because people are unemployed and have to phanda to eat. Although you are not obliged to give these people money, you often feel it's the right thing to do to maintain a sense of neighbourliness. It also ensures that your family will be protected and won't become victim to crime, gossip or hatred.

Now, if toll gates or e-toll were called black tax, I would not have any problem with it. It would deserve the name of being a tax, which you are forced to pay whether you want to or not.

Part of me wants to blame a particular sector of the black middle class for giving our noble gesture of family upliftment so bad a name as 'black tax'. Then again, if we look at the origins of the term in South Africa, it does become easier to understand how it gained traction and started getting a negative undertone.

'Black tax' seems to have its origins in the late 2000s, when the black middle class were among the hardest hit by the recession. They were repaying study loans to the banks and TEFSA (Tertiary Education Fund of South Africa), paying instalments on their cars, preparing for marriage and in turn paying ilobolo, extending the family house by building more rooms, moving out of the family house and renting in an expensive suburb closer to work, buying a new house in developing sections of the township or in an expensive suburb and so forth.

Furthermore, these black professionals were expected to look after a brother and sister who were still in high school or their disadvantaged sister's child who had been abandoned by his father. All of this, together with the scourge of unemployment in our communities, turned into a sore which refused to heal.

Joburg life had begun to choke the black middle class. Like a hustler they had to touch here and touch there in their struggle to survive, but given their resilience they carried on for as long as possible.

In light of this economic throttle, many members of the black middle class felt they needed to move away from the traditional way of life. They needed something to give them the courage, determination, self-confidence and will to put some distance between themselves and what they called 'the trappings of communal family values'. The first thing they did was to unintentionally demonise the idea of family upliftment by calling it some kind of tax – black tax.

What used to be known as family upliftment now became 'family on family violence'. Suddenly, it was viewed as an abusive cultural practice, a burden on black people's progress, a stress and a pain, a drain on limited resources, an imposition by the family elders, and so on. And so black tax got a negative connotation.

In her MBA research project titled, 'Black tax: The emerging middle class reality', scholar Nonhlanhla Magubane contends that 'black tax refers to both the social and economic support, such as money, shelter, food, and clothing, indicating that the middle class provides to their extended family or kinship network'. She also suggests that black tax is enabled by both external factors (high inequality and unemployment levels) and internal factors (a broken family structure where there was a divorce or death of a parent).

According to Magubane there are two schools of thought in the debate about the meaning of 'black tax'. The first school describes it as 'a deeper societal level of discrimination, and continued inequality as a result of the legacy of apartheid that the majority of South Africans still face'. The second school 'focuses on financial obligations that the black middle class have towards their extended family members as a result of continued inequality caused by the apartheid legacy'.[1]

I agree with both definitions since they point to the exact knot in time and place where this noble gesture of ubuntu is located. However, I have a problem with the term 'black tax'.

For me this gesture should be called 'family upliftment', and it should be traced to the place where the past, the present and the future of our entire universe as communal African people are tied together. An African person who tries to circumvent this communal life that we inherited from our ancestors as family responsibility is like a tree without roots.

I lost my father in 1989 when I was 16 years old. At that point my mother had never taken a job before. She was a housewife looking after her ten kids. When my father died, the responsibility of looking after us fell on my two employed brothers.

They had no choice because the only way to keep the spirits of our culture alive was to perform this duty of looking after us. Failing in these obligations would mean that our ancestral spirits, who planted the seed of continuity in our families, would be tied to useless, corporeal bodies. If this happened, our family would lose its legacy because no ancestral soul had been kept alive and thus the spirits could not be guided to return to the communal family structure.

To me, this represents the natural cycle of African life. It ensures that family roots and communal structure are not destroyed by the so-called alien civilisation of an individualistic lifestyle.

When I was growing up in Soweto my parents accommodated a number of extended family members in our tiny four-roomed house. Most of them came from far-off rural areas looking for a job in Johannesburg. Our house belonged to our extended family members as well. It never even crossed our minds that we were sacrificing our space and freedom.

The conditions under apartheid also forced people to be

communal. For example, due to influx control a person could not leave the rural areas freely and go to the urban areas to look for a job. You had to have a reference or family in the city you were visiting or else you would be branded as an illegal immigrant by the apartheid authorities and jailed. Most people got their jobs because they were referred by their family members. Several of our family members were appointed at the place where my father used to work. This way of life also helped to keep us as far away as possible from the master's kick.

I doubt that these relatives were black-taxing my father. My father was simply uplifting his family so that they would be able to uplift others. This is the cycle of responsibility within a family. In fact, my father used to embrace this by saying, 'Only alien creatures are devoid of human pity. By giving, your mind will cooperate fully with your soul. We are just like a communal village, and that's our nature.'

I strongly believe this is the spirit that has taught us to be adaptable even when faced with negative, hostile circumstances. We have learnt to find joy and happiness in situations where other people might be discouraged because we know there will always be the communal safety net.

In 1997, I left Wits University to study law at the University of Cape Town. My cousin helped me with the registration money and gave me R250 in pocket money for about four months, until my bursary and stipend were approved. Back then, he was a factory worker and had two children to support. He is one of the relatives who had come to stay in our house for years when my father was still alive.

My cousin was retrenched in 2010, the same year in which

his son passed matric. At the time, I had a well-paying job, so I decided to take on the responsibility of sending my cousin's son to the Johannesburg Technical College to do the N3 Engineering programme. I also managed to secure a bursary for him. Today, he works for a big engineering company, earning a good salary, and I'm very proud of this.

Of course, this doesn't mean that the tradition or system of family upliftment is not open to abuse. Like any system based on love and trust, it will always be abused by some family members for selfish reasons. When this happens, it qualifies to be called black tax.

A friend of mine who works in Cape Town told me of how he and his mother had a terrible fight when, for a year, he had been giving her money so she could buy building material to extend their family house. He revealed to me that his mother used the money to gamble in fafi or mchaina and the Lotto and also used it for payments to her stokvel. On top of this, she has been blackmailing him emotionally by saying he should forget about family blessings if he ever gets married and has children. He has since stopped coming home to Johannesburg.

Some people believe it is their duty to beget children so that they, the children, can look after them when they're old. These beliefs are common in many African communities. Unfortunately, in some cases it perpetuates a cycle of exploitation because the child's life is not seen to be his own: he merely exists to link his parents to their ancestors. These parents behave like ticks and suck their children dry. In this way they enslave the souls of their children.

A lady friend of mine recently told me how she was blackmailed into taking over her mother's account from a clothing shop. Her mother is a grant recipient, yet she had a clothing account at a well-known retail shop that eventually blacklisted her. She also owed loan sharks thousands of rands and my lady friend had to pay for this, as well as her own student loans and other debts.

Family members convinced her that if she did not help her mother, her ancestors would cast a spell on her so that she would not get married and have children. Not having children and getting married is a big issue in African communities and my lady friend buckled under the pressure.

Parents shouldn't hold their children to ransom. When they are abused in this way, the channel through which the spirit of family upliftment must flow is blocked. It shouldn't become an unfair burden or make it impossible for people to save money for themselves.

Apart from this kind of abuse, the system of family upliftment can sometimes also encourage dependency. I've had friends whose families were well-off and could therefore afford to give them a decent monthly stipend. Many of them amounted to nothing and still depend on their families. Some have become drug addicts, a habit financed by this monthly allowance.

Guilt tripping should not be part of the system of family upliftment. No, it's not my duty to educate my siblings unless my parents are dead. We should not feel forced to help our family members; the offer should come freely. For me, assisting my family has a soothing effect. It creates a feeling of peacefulness. I've realised that ignoring the responsibility to help family members when I am in a position to do so causes a kind of illness in my spirit that no doctor has yet found a cure for. I become more prone to worry and fear and I feel as if I'm losing my cultural support structure.

So, how do we avoid letting 'black tax' enslave us in spirit and in flesh, turning us into empty shells? In informal conversation with a few people, I've heard a number of useful suggestions.

Firstly, some people say, we must plan. We have to be honest with our immediate family (parents and siblings) about our earning potential and only take on as much responsibility as we can afford. We need to effectively balance our needs and those of our immediate family. We should not try to be superheroes because we can't save everyone. Most importantly, we must always remember to reward ourselves for waking up every day to work in a hostile environment where we are probably still paid less than we deserve because of our gender, race or both.

Secondly, we can look for opportunities to earn extra income, like having a second job or a business on the side. From this perspective, it will help us to do more for others and ourselves. However, you should be careful not to overcommit yourself and die of stress in the process, especially if your family isn't aware of the pressure you are under. In most black communities, once you drive a car, you're considered rich and viewed as a walking ATM. The moment you tell your family you cannot help them, it's interpreted as being selfish.

Thirdly, some say we must give a fixed amount to our parents every month or two and create a situation where any sibling who needs money can talk to them about it. People who subscribe to this way of doing things say we should be proud when we help educate our nephews and nieces. Their success is our success and the gratitude they show towards us for helping them out gives us a sense of fulfilment.

Still, they warn of their fear of being marginalised when they don't meet the larger family demands. This is when what they call emotional tax comes into play. They also point out that there are adult family members who are just too happy to be complacent and don't contribute anything.

Fourthly, there are those who say we need to create generational wealth to perform our family obligations in a natural way and be rid of 'black tax'. They believe this is the only way to ensure our (future) families don't have to go through the same thing we are having to cope with. They argue that if we acknowledged our cultural identity and practices of looking after each other, we wouldn't even call it black tax. According to this argument, we have been taking care of each other for generations in the family. We have to embrace this part of our culture.

For example, you can help to build a small spaza shop or hire a jumping castle for one of the children's parties as some kind of empowerment. A friend in Soweto also told me how he bought four hair clippers for his brother, who today is a successful hairdresser. By doing so, he put his brother in a position to start making his own money.

What everyone I spoke to agreed on was that one must be careful of family members who want to budget for you. Don't let anyone bully you. You must define what you want to inherit as your family responsibility.

Choose carefully between sibling education, home renovations, funeral cover, a monthly allowance and a contribution towards a good and proper stokvel. Charity begins at home, but we still have to prioritise. For example, if your family live in a shack, you obviously first have to build a house for them.

The term 'black tax' remains fundamentally flawed. It is a problematic expression that needs to be interrogated before the filthy smoke it emits starts to choke us. It doesn't give us a truthful foundation on which to base our family obligations and it goes against the concept of ubuntu. It's supposed to be something good, yet the term connotes something unethical, improper or evil.

'Black tax' has the negative connotations of a phrase like 'clever blacks', which is used to define an educated black person who criticises the so-called black authority but cowers before the white man. It forces us to imagine our lives through the prism of colonial modernity that has no memory of our culture.

'Black tax' also seems to imply that breaking away from entrenched family values is equal to escaping to a larger, freer society. It preaches a false consciousness that there is a completeness and a deeper and more comprehending love to be found when we abandon our supposedly 'high maintenance' families. Such a false belief will make it difficult for future generations to develop a vital and effective belief in the past as part of our present concerns, or the present as a consequence of the past's concerns.

For all these reasons I think we should call our system 'family upliftment' instead of 'black tax'. I return to the immortality of the family soul: I believe that the present has its roots firmly planted in the past and that helping my family in the present life will help to guide my soul to return to its roots in the next life.

NIQ MHLONGO is a Sowetan-born writer and a travel journalist who has written three novels and two collections of short stories. He has facilitated creative writing workshops around the world, judged the Dinaane Debut Fiction Award in 2017 and curated the Time of the Writer Festival in 2019. He is the City Editor of the *Johannesburg Review of Books*. Niq was also the creative force behind picking the name for the Maboneng Precinct in Johannesburg in 2009.

Note

1 Magubane, NN. 'Black tax: The emerging middle class reality', MBA dissertation. University of Pretoria, 2016.

Compassion

Angela Makholwa

When I think of black South Africans as a homogeneous entity, the words that come to mind are resilience, hope, tenacity and ubuntu.

Ubuntu. A beautiful word that captures the spirit of our people despite losing some of its resonance thanks to Castle Lite advertisements. Ubuntu is what makes me most proud of being a black South African – in the sense that I'm never alone; not in hours of deep despair or at the exhilarating heights of my greatest triumphs.

'The word ubuntu is derived from a Nguni (isiZulu) aphorism: Umuntu Ngumuntu Ngabantu, which can be translated as "a person is a person because of or through others". Ubuntu can be described as the capacity in an African culture to express compassion, reciprocity, dignity, humanity and mutuality in the interests of building and maintaining communities with justice and mutual caring,' Courage Kusemwa and Emmanuel Mandidzidze write in an article entitled 'Ubuntu Philosophy: An Old Solution for Contemporary Problems'.

They go on to say: 'an African is not a rugged individual, but a person living within a community. In a hostile environment, it is only through such community solidarity that hunger, isolation, deprivation, poverty and any emerging challenges can be survived, because of the community's brotherly and sisterly concern, cooperation, care, and sharing.'

Many cultural practices are underpinned by the philosophy of ubuntu, yet there seems to be a movement to erode or do away with these practices because of the impact they have on people's pockets.

For instance, in black culture, if there is a death in someone's family, the community will spend the days leading up to the funeral visiting the family of the deceased to be present in their time of grieving. I choose the word 'present' because that is essentially what the practice requires of the visitors – simply to be there. Sometimes it might be in silent communion, at others to sing hymns to console and soothe the pain of loss experienced by the grieving family, or, in other instances, visitors may share words of comfort.

This is a typical act of compassion that is now under attack because of the pressure on the bereaved family to cater for the constant stream of visitors. Having personally experienced this practice, however, I know that some visitors will bring cakes and treats, or even groceries, because they are aware of these expectations. This in itself is a further example of ubuntu in practice.

Why then is there this growing clarion call to do away with practices that are the hallmarks of our humanity and compassion as a people? Perhaps our walled-in lives in town-house complexes and imposing estates make us feel removed from the plight of our fellow beings. Or are we so glad to have made our way out of the townships and villages of our origins that we have become desperate to assimilate to western culture and want to dissociate ourselves from anything that reminds us of who we are and where we come from?

I am astounded that after centuries of systemic oppression, those of us who have managed to make something of our lives are now in such turmoil over this so-called black tax and the supposed imposition on our wallets. Why are we even calling it 'black tax'? Does taking care of kin and kind now feel like an albatross around our necks?

I despise the cynicism of the term and hate how it sounds like an escape from something. What are we running away from? And if the tax is specifically black, does it mean we want to be free of it in order to emulate our lighter-hued brethren? Do we now want to travel light, free of all this burden?

Let me qualify my opinion by delving into my own personal experience of 'black tax'. I was raised in Emkhathini, a middle-class neighbourhood in Tembisa, on the East Rand of Johannesburg. My mother was a nursing sister and my father was a high-school teacher. Growing up, I had a tight-knit circle of friends whose parents were also professionals, mostly in teaching, nursing or similar backgrounds.

When we were pursuing our studies at institutions of higher learning, a friend's mother passed away, after which her father promptly sold their childhood home and left both my friend and her brother to fend for themselves. This brutal decision sent their lives on a completely different trajectory to that of their peers. While most of us went on to complete our studies and pursue professional careers, my friend was stuck in limbo, with no access to the resources the rest of us enjoyed.

Within a few years, my friend had become despondent, working in informal jobs, and eventually ended up staying in rented backrooms in our township. She would periodically request money from me and another friend, Ntombi (not her real name), until this became a sort of monthly expectation. I could not accept the change in her circumstances and was broken-hearted over how her life had derailed.

The payment requests went on for a while till Ntombi decided to find a long-term solution to our mutual friend's predicament. We agreed to pool our resources to register her for a nursing course. Much to our surprise, our friend told us that nursing would be 'career suicide' for her; this from someone who had no discernible source of employment at the time.

I can imagine you thinking, 'There you go, this is what happens when people get accustomed to handouts'. But I cite this example because, up to that point, I had not felt overly burdened by my friend's requests for money because I knew that she needed it. She was a single mother at the time – as was I, by the way – and I understood the financial strain she was under.

After she declined our offer to assist with the course, we decided that we had gone as far as we could to help lighten her burden. Admittedly, we were quite disappointed with her stance, but at least we knew that we had tried our best to make life easier for her.

Helping someone who is in dire straits should be second nature to us all. It's what makes us human. Sure, some people take advantage of acts of kindness, but nothing stops you from calling it out once it presents itself. Surely, that cannot be a reason for us to agitate to stop being compassionate towards family or friends in need.

Let us not emulate the self-appointed 'Prophets of Profit'

who muddy our social media walls with posts like 'Poverty is a choice' and 'Don't respect a man who begs on the street because anyone can hustle for that million'. We all know that life does not work like that.

The breast-beating declarations of snake oil salesmen who peddle lies disguised as 'motivational talks' seek to diminish the plight of those who are trapped in a genuine cycle of poverty by citing cleverly edited stories of how these wily entrepreneurs managed to pull themselves up and now own successful businesses and drive posh cars. These types usually end their talks by making comments like, 'I did it, so what are you waiting for?'

Suddenly, everyone is self-made and those who don't have the means to take the first step out of the poverty cycle are social pariahs who are simply too lazy to use their brains and are 'busy waiting for handouts'.

Very rarely will such a shining example of entrepreneurship and commerce share stories of how Mme Lerato next door loaned him R30 so that he could catch a taxi to go to the interview that set the wheels of his success in motion. Or how he was short of R2 000 to register for his stockbroker licence and was saved by his sister, who transferred her last R2 000 so that he could have a start in life.

Every man or woman who bemoans the burden of 'black tax' is in fact a little boy or girl who suffers from a mild form of amnesia. They've forgotten the little favours they garnered from friends, neigbours and family, which eventually led them to where they are now.

Remember that time you were introduced to an uncle you'd never heard of, who was kind enough to let you bunk at his rented apartment so that you could have better access to your campus at Wits while your parents scrounged around for your residence fees? Or the time your mother's burial society loaned your family money so you could register for university since you did not qualify for the National Student Financial Aid Scheme (NSFAS)?

The truth is that for centuries, black South Africans have battled to access finance through traditional means. Banks have never loved the colour black. Even with banks using artificial intelligence to remove human bias from credit decisions, banks still don't love the colour black.

Because of systemic oppression, most of us don't have rich uncles who own businesses where we can temp during the holidays to raise extra cash. I'm yet to meet a black friend who is a trust fund baby . . . Maybe I just don't have many friends who come from political families or I don't have the privilege of being friends with rich kids, but the truth is, for most black people, all they can rely on in times of financial need is their friends and families.

Most black South Africans have friends or family who still live in abject poverty. You only need to spend an hour in any given township or village to register the fact that the dream of a so-called Rainbow Nation has not trickled down to the places where it is most needed.

Let's be honest, most of these black tax amounts are minimal compared to our earnings. A typical request is for R500 to R1 000; I guess that's another reason why it's called black tax. If you're Patrice Motsepe, I suppose the request will go up to about R50 000.

So now, after 20 odd years of democracy, some of us are

privileged enough to live in the 'burbs and drive around in our bank-loaned vehicles, but we feel burdened to send R500 to the niece who needs taxi money to get to campus!

There's no such thing as black tax. When you are asked to help someone you care about and have the resources to do so, you go ahead and help them. It's simple. It's called compassion.

ANGELA MAKHOLWA is a fiction writer based in Johannesburg. Her previous works include *Red Ink*, a gritty crime thriller about the relationship that develops between a journalist and the serial killer she is doing research on for a book. Also in Angela's oeuvre are *The 30th Candle, Black Widow Society* and her latest novel, *The Blessed Girl*, which tells the story of a young woman who manipulates her older, married lovers to access a life of luxury and designer brands.

Black tax and the art of investing

Bhekisisa Mncube

There has been a lot of breast-beating and brouhaha around the notion of 'black tax'. According to the 'woke' generation, this is a colloquial term used to describe young black people – especially males – who share their after-tax income with immediate and extended family members, while they are expected to manage their own expenses, which may include purchasing a nice car and/or a house.

Apparently, only a quarter of South Africans between the ages of 18 and 30 are saving for retirement. This is according to the Old Mutual Savings and Investment Monitor, which also claims this happens because they (middle-income blacks) use their income to support extended families, instead of putting away some of their hard-earned money. Unfortunately, this definition and attendant explanation are ahistorical and not really helpful; neither are the statistics.

I prefer to view so-called black tax as a modern form of family investment for the future of the clan. As commentator Sifiso Mkhonto writes in a column, black tax 'is a responsibility, not a burden'.

As the history of South Africa tells us, the imposition of various taxes by the authorities forced black people off their ancestral land and drove them to seek employment in the cities at a very low wage. As most jobs were in the cities and since wage levels could not support entire families, black males became migrant labourers, leaving wives and mothers in charge of the rural household. Females, children and the elderly would have to survive as best they could on remittances and whatever crops and livestock they were able to cultivate.

Crispin Phiri, a candidate attorney at a Johannesburg law firm, was quoted in a *Mail & Guardian* article as saying he finds the term 'black tax' apt. 'Black tax is very real and is an exclusively black experience . . . You are brought up to first look out for your family; you can't be living in luxury while your family struggles.'

Phiri, a 26-year-old, lives with his mother and pays his 17-year-old sister's school fees. 'I understand that we are an unequal society and this is the one way of addressing that inequality so that the next generation is better off than we were, and can live a life that is fairly more comfortable than ours.'

While Phiri understands the genesis of 'black tax' he doesn't take into account the full historical basis of it. The truth of the matter is that black tax is a result of the colonial administration and, later, the apartheid regime.

The first egregious land grabs in South Africa began on 6 April 1652, with the arrival of a Dutch national, one Jan van Riebeeck. According to South African History Online, white colonial land dispossession began at the Cape with the expansion of the Dutch colonial settlement established by Van Riebeeck on behalf of the Dutch East India Company. Initially, he was authorised to set up a refreshment station for the company's ships, but with the need for a more sustainable source of meat and vegetable supply, more land was required.

This is the original sin and the genesis of 'black tax'. As a result, land was seized from the Khoikhoi, and later the San, to increase Dutch grazing pastures, expand their farming activities and establish settlements. Over time, the reduction of grazing pastures traditionally used by the Khoikhoi resulted in conflict between them and the Dutch. Eventually, the Dutch defeated the Khoikhoi and expropriated more of their land. Deprived of their livelihood, they were forced to seek employment on the farmlands of white colonial settlers.

Before the arrival of the colonialists, black South Africans had a viable family support structure. Men hunted for meat and ploughed fields, boys looked after livestock, and women collected wood and cooked. In fact, it was quite a simple structure. But it worked. Everybody had a role to play in the sustenance of the family unit. Most importantly, nobody starved. And nobody survived on handouts.

A century or two after Van Riebeeck's arrival, it came to pass that a generation of black males were forced to work far away from their homes to support their families in the rural villages. Because women and children were not allowed to work, the men became the sole breadwinners. This was the beginning of 'black tax'. Women and children in the villages were eager to till the land for a living, but it couldn't support them fully because often the land was barren. So, they all depended on the working male figure in the family for material support.

At some stage, the apartheid government and even most of the major mining companies decided that their brutal policies should be extended to whole (black) families. They implemented a South African version of the 'grandfather-father clause'. This meant that a family member of working age was guaranteed a job if one of their older family members worked on the mines, in manufacturing or in the quasi-black governments of the so-called homelands.

For instance, my eldest brother (born from my father's relationship with another woman before he married my mother and I was born) worked on the mines. When he came into our lives at over 30 years of age, he encouraged us to join him on the Johannesburg mines where he worked. We never did. However, a number of my peers did join the mining industry because their kin worked there. For some odd reason, I was always attracted to academic pursuits.

For all these reasons the concept of 'black tax' can be traced back to the colonial/apartheid state in South Africa. No black person chose it; it was imposed by the material conditions of the time.

Fast forward to 1993: I become the first person in the Mncube family, out of some nine households, to undertake tertiary education. In this endeavour, I was financed by the Germans through the Ecumenical Bursary Fund. I was both revered and loathed. My family thought I was special, but our neighbours thought otherwise. They said I was destined for failure because I had too much pride. They firmly believed that pride comes before a fall. Well, they were wrong.

Because my bursary paid only for tuition fees, my second-eldest sister bought me essential books worth R600. In fact, she became the first person in the Mncube family of Eshowe to pay the dreaded 'black tax' and, as such, is case study number 1. She was working part-time at the then Sales House department store. Although she had completed her matric, she didn't proceed to tertiary education due to a lack of financial resources. To this day, she hasn't acquired any post-matric qualification. However, she is a resourceful and financially independent woman.

Years later, my younger (last-born) sister completed her matric. It was now my turn to pay 'black tax'. She registered for a commerce degree at the University of KwaZulu-Natal. I paid for her upkeep, including accommodation and food. After an unbroken four years of academic study, she completed her degree and secured a job at the same university.

Today, my younger sister is an important and financially independent member of the Mncube family – case study 2. She has since secured a bursary and completed her honours degree in Supply Chain Management. When she got married, I was naturally asked by my father to help with the expenses associated with marriage.

Case study 3: my sister who was born after me had volunteered at the South African Police Service (SAPS) for five years. During her fifth year, she was told that police trainee posts had become available, and she was encouraged to apply. But there was a snag. She didn't have a valid driver's licence. At the time, this was a non-negotiable requirement to be enlisted as a trainee police officer.

She phoned me at once. At the time I was unemployed after being retrenched by a big JSE-listed company. However, I had saved my pension pay-out in order to complete my postgraduate studies. As soon as my sister phoned and explained her predicament, I was sold. I gave her enough money to obtain her driver's licence. Months later, she was enlisted as a police officer trainee. Two years later, she completed her training and became a full member of SAPS.

It has been ten years since I paid for her driver's licence and she has had a successful career in the police force. In the intervening years, it became apparent that she was ready to get married. According to our isiZulu culture, someone had to fund the many isiZulu ceremonies that are associated with marriage. Because I was still the only male member of the Mncube family with a job, my father instructed me to become my sister's benefactor. I paid a total of R40 000 for 11 ilobolo cows to be registered in my name. After the compulsory slaughtering of cows for various ceremonies, I was left with only four cows.

Over the years, I have sold some of my cows to pay for my son's education. My 14-year-old daughter goes to a private high school. Her mother and I are jointly responsible to her fees.

Case study 4: I have even supported a second generation of the Mncube clan. My eldest brother was murdered in 2001. At the time of his death, he was a master's student at the then University of Natal. He is survived by three children. It was par for the course that I had to support his children financially and otherwise.

My brother's eldest daughter is currently pursuing her master's in technology at the Durban University of Technology. As a result of her excellent academic record, she is also a junior academic in her department. I supported her from her days as an undergraduate student until she secured funding from the National Student Financial Aid Scheme – which never paid enough at the time, though.

Case study 5: my brother's other daughter failed matric. After a family discussion and negotiations, it was agreed that she should go to a fee-paying high school outside our village to complete her matric. This meant she had to repeat Grades 11 and 12. So, for two years, I had to pay for her studies – from tuition fees and accommodation, to food and travel. Today she is a student at the University of South Africa and no longer funded by me.

Case study 6: my brother's only son is now a third-year medical student at the University of KwaZulu-Natal. I supported him for a number of years during high school by sending money to my maternal family. However, thanks to his excellent academic record – which ensured that he obtained a full bursary for his first year at varsity – and support from his mother, he has needed the least support from me. These days, I occasionally buy him airtime, data and food on request.

In 2019, all the beneficiaries of the 'black tax' in our family are helping my father and mother. My mom is the happiest beneficiary of 'black tax.' As the only working son, it's my duty to send her an allowance to supplement her pension.

For big ticket items, we (the black tax beneficiaries) all contribute according to what we can afford. For instance, in December 2018, we crowdfunded to purchase an electric stove for my parents. Two years before, we had crowdfunded to renovate our parents' bedroom and bought them a queen bed, new sheets, pillows, etc.

Of course there is always a black sheep or two in the family. For these fellows, no amount of investment yields any benefits.

As these case studies from our family demonstrate, 'black tax' is not a burden. In fact, it must be one of the best financial investments in the modern black family. Every cent that is spent to help a family member has a multiplier effect on the rest of the family and they will benefit in the years to come.

BHEKISISA MNCUBE is an author and former journalist. He lives in Pretoria with a couple of loving women, a persistent hangover and a couple of regrets.

Andizi! Black tax is a flawed social construct

Phehello J Mofokeng

I grew up in the backwaters of Bethlehem, in the Free State, on simple principles – perhaps it is because we did not have much in our family.

My father was born in 1948, the year apartheid was legislated, a different time. In 1969 he walked through one of the biggest snowfalls in South Africa, barefoot. He left school after Form 1 (Grade 8) despite being an excellent pupil who attained a first-class pass. My father did not have any opportunities after leaving school.

Together, he and I are building a house right now, in the Free State. This is not black tax.

My father and mother were domestic workers and today I am a university graduate. In their twilight years, who am I supposed to hand them over to? These are old people who did not have any financial opportunities, let alone financial education. I mean, my parents never earned enough to save for anything in the first place.

My father receives an allowance from me – not because he ever asked for it; on the contrary he hates that I do this for him. He says I have my own family and that my first responsibility should be them. But this is our agreement: he gets electricity, airtime and an allowance based on what I can afford. I treat him to expensive restaurant experiences when my family and I visit him – and this is not a tax. It is a social pact that I have with him and my family.

My father has always propounded this very basic principle: you cannot eat when others are not eating. That is to say, you cannot enjoy luxuries with impunity while others wallow in lack. This is how and why I know that what I am doing is merely part of my self-preservation.

What is 'black tax', anyway? It is a foreign concept to me even though it is increasingly bandied about. Its narrative is wrong – for me at least – because it is premised on the selfish, capitalist attitude of 'me first' and I was not raised that way. I therefore reject it with contempt.

When I went to university, my brother – who started working right after college – supported me during the difficult financial patches. Today, we both have children. His child is mine and mine are his. This is not a burden or a tax – it is a duty that we perform for each other as blood brothers, as family. So, no, andizi! I do not believe helping your siblings or your parents is a taxation of any sort.

It is possible for us – for this generation of young professionals – to adopt a toxic narrative around this matter, especially if it's being advanced by the media. We are a generation that grew up on TV and few books. We are educated, yet we often lack imagination. Therefore, anything we are told repeatedly seeps in easily and we consume anything that comes through those screens, even the toxic stuff. The narrative of black tax is exactly that, a toxic, nonsensical missive that we believe without any critical analysis.

There are many different experiences around this social construct called black tax, but a distinction must be made between forking out for lavish luxuries and helping with bare necessities. There is a difference between buying school textbooks or taking care of your orphaned batjhana (nieces and nephews) and being blackmailed into paying for lavish lifestyles by family members.

Sadly, some of us have allowed our families to abuse our status and professional standing. Siblings that refuse to work demand luxurious items we can barely afford, often merely for bragging rights, and we acquiesce. They get you to pay for useless things such as DStv, liquor, expensive parties or 'slaying' – just so that they can be viewed a certain way by their neighbours.

Buying luxury goods for your siblings is not 'black tax' – it is you being taken advantage of, especially if you cannot afford it. It is different from fixing your parents' home, putting your deserving siblings through school, or paying for a destitute family member's funeral. Getting into debt to do it is not taxation, it is stupidity! As a professional and educated person who understands personal finance, you are supposed to know better.

We feel the pressure to fulfil such nonsensical whims when we do not have a clear social pact in place with our families. My family knows where I cut the umbilical cord – and that is at the essentials.

Materialism and wanting to compete with your peers in terms of financial success fuels the social construct of 'black tax'. If we were not competing with the Joneses and Mokoenas from next door over a new house, a new car or better and bigger cellphones, then helping to build better futures for and with our families would not seem like a burden.

If you call it black tax, it means you expect something in return. When you pay taxes, you get something for it – roads, infrastructure and whatever government does with taxes these days. When you help your siblings because your parents have no income and no savings, do you do so with an expectation of sorts? If so, then you are correct in viewing this as a tax. But what I do for family members – up to a reasonable limit – is not owed to me.

Indeed, this is a matter of matsoho a ya hlatswana, one hand washes the other and re tjhabana sa kgomo, we are a nation of the same cow (hide). Matsoho a ya hlatswana does not mean providing for luxuries to your family, especially when you cannot afford it – that is a perversion of idioms.

Sesotho is rife with concepts of nationhood, a sense of community and family structure. It is sad to see these concepts being perverted by academics, the media and some demanding family members who feel entitled to our 'success'. I am repulsed by how some academics have distorted the old adages of botho (ubuntu) to justify and further sell this social construct of 'black tax'. Many have accepted this perversion of who we are without much critical thought, even though these are not just idioms, but capture the essence of who we are.

'Black tax' is an ill-informed, flawed social construct that I reject. I see it as misguided and ill-informed academisation and mainstreaming of black people's struggles.

I was raised to believe that we should take care of each

other. If our parents are considered a burden, mine is one I carry with pride. For me it is a badge of honour.

As part of my pact with my father he knows my salary and what I have to spend it on. He realises that city life is expensive and this has mitigated his expectations of me, to the extent that he sometimes refuses my acts of goodwill. It is all because I have set limits to what I can afford and what I can't. If we can all reach this point, we will soon realise that our parents are not financially illiterate; that they know how money works and are often reasonable.

When she died at around 106 years old, my great-grandmother was living with us in an arrangement that you would consider part of 'black tax'. She raised my father when my grandmother remarried, leaving my father behind and so utterly destitute that he had to give up his promising educational prospects.

Today, many grandparents and great-grandparents are confined to unloving, sterile and foreign old-age homes – just so their children can live in comfort and luxury. If you view taking care of your parents as any form of taxation, then you will find nothing wrong in sending them to an old-age home.

I am building a house for my father. It is my wife who encouraged me to do this and there are many reasons. Firstly, I do not want him to end up in an old-age home. Secondly, in terms of our culture, my children's umbilical cords are supposed to be buried in the soil of my ancestral home. As white people still refuse us land, I cannot do this in Joburg, as one has to sell a kidney, a liver and two hearts to afford land in this place.

My only option is to build a cultural and traditional base

for myself – for my children. This is best done on my father's property in the township of Bohlokong. As taxing as this responsibility is, it is an act of self-preservation. When the house is complete my children will have a piece of land to bury the umbilical cords of their own children. While this might not be a big deal to many Africans in the city, it is crucial to those of us who come from a traditional and cultural upbringing.

Paying for the basics in my family gives me a sense of responsibility, of 'adulting'. It also gives me status in my family – not because of my material wealth, but because I know where my father comes from. In his twilight years, I am his pillar. He has been mine since the day I was born.

I will not honour my father with empty gestures of expensive tombstones and caskets after his death, but now, with my presence, laughter, love and, yes, with my limited funds, too. He is my living ancestor, my older brother, the guardian of my children, and if he is a tax, he is one that I accept wholly and willingly.

PHEHELLO MOFOKENG is the author of *Sankomota: An Ode in One Album* and a multi-dimensional artist with over ten years' publishing and media experience. He is an organising committee member of the Franschhoek Literary Festival and an MA student at Wits. Phehello has worked for some of South Africa's most successful television programmes, including *Isibaya, Isithembiso and Curious Culture*. His Sesotho novella will be released in 2019.

It's a black thing

Primrose Mrwebi

Black tax is very much like the land issue – every time you mention it, it's as if you are saying a swear word. The more you try to explain the complexities around it, the more some people feel offended. Ironically, the people who put us in this position, of having to pay black tax, are the ones who struggle the most to get the concept.

I got my first taste of black tax when I was in high school and started waiting tables at a fast-paced restaurant in Cape Town's southern suburbs. The money I earned was not a lot, but it paid for the basics I needed as a 16-year-old. The tips at the end of each shift definitely made my life comfortable.

At the time, my mother was working as a helper for the Malan family, who were based in Claremont, which was fairly close to the restaurant. After my shift I would go to their house so my mother and I could travel home, to Khayelitsha, together. It was a trip of about 45 minutes and cost R18 one way. We got home so late that we would only have time to eat and then go directly to sleep. Most of my hard-earned money would be spent on transport – I hated that.

There was always this unspoken agreement that whatever amount you made, you would share with your mother and siblings or any relative and neighbours who came asking. This was quite annoying, but it was drilled into me by my mother as a form of good manners. Little did I know how these first experiences of black tax during my teenage years would follow me into adulthood.

After high school, I went to theatre school to study for a degree in speech and drama. I continued waitressing for the duration of my degree. Fortunately, I made much more money because I was working at a high-end restaurant and I also stayed at a residence in town and could walk to work.

I still contributed at home, giving most of my salary away, and each time we went to our village of Mceula, near Queenstown in the Eastern Cape, I knew I had to have a lot of money so I could help out my extended family. After all, they were my cousins, uncles and aunts. They were always so cheerful and welcoming at our arrival, showing us around as if we did not know the place even though we visited every year. This was very endearing and still is. Nevertheless, we also knew that money played a big part.

While I was studying, I had also started dating. However, I only had time to go on dates on the weekend because when you study speech and drama, your day begins at nine in the morning and ends at six in the afternoon; when you have a production on, you rarely get to bed before midnight. On weekends I was back in the township to see my loved ones. That meant that for a date, I would have to take two taxis to travel from my mother's house to get to town; so, by the time we went half-and-half on the bill, I had spent three times more money than the other person. Eish.

I did not want to be one of those black people who cannot

pay their own bill but I also realised that none of my white friends knew that I had to save for when we went to the village, or that most of my money was spent helping siblings and family members, or even just a neighbour who had run out of electricity or didn't have bus fare to go to work the next day.

After I started my professional career and found a proper job that came with a payslip, I had to start repaying my first-year study loan. My earnings were now divided by three – there was my debt and my personal needs, then there was my family and, lastly, there was my extended family and friends, like Aunty Nono, whose baby daddy could not pay papgeld so she came to my mother every week to share our groceries.

Black tax follows you everywhere because the more money you earn, the more you are expected give. Some family members even go as far as asking you how much you earn per month, which I find to be such an invasion of privacy. Luckily, I have learnt to talk my way out of those questions. I always say I don't really work because I do the things I love – that answer always gets me out of trouble!

Sometimes black tax even follows us into our marital homes. There are in-laws who expect you to contribute to them the same way you do to your own immediate family, because when a black woman gets married, she marries into her husband's family: there is a saying that we marry the spouse's family too, so now you have double the trouble.

A friend of mine is expected to pay a family allowance to her mother in-law, even though her husband has passed away. She still does this, every month. She laments the fact that he was such an abusive cheat, but her mother-in-law still refers to her as 'our makoti', so she feels obliged to pay. I feel sorry for her, but it is her choice and her business.

If you have a helper in your household you also have to help her family, which means you often end up doing for her what you would do for both your families. So, brace yourself. You might need to pay for her children's school fees or for her trip to the village and try to pay her some kind of bonus at the end of the year.

This sense of responsibility one feels towards one's helper is something many people don't understand, simply because they are not in our shoes. This story is deep and layered but it comes down to us taking responsibility.

One evening, over drinks, I told one of my white friends how I had paid for bus tickets for my helper and also bought her a sheep and groceries when her son returned from initiation school. My friend told me I was crazy to do so and that I simply liked to carry other people's burdens. She said the fact that I paid my helper well should be enough. It was an issue she chose not to understand. Afterwards, she uttered the most offensive comments about black people. Needless to say, that was the end of our drinks night and the end of our friendship.

As with the matter of land, some people choose not to see why black tax is a burning issue for us as black people or how much some of us are like 'Uncle Msholi' – the former president – in wanting things we did not work for. While I have worked for every dime I have ever earned, I also feel South Africa has deliberately made us disadvantaged and, as such, we will always have certain problems that white people will not. It's so unfair.

Some people might think talking about the pros and cons of black tax is a tiring debate, but it is one that we must have. Do I hate black tax? Yes, sometimes I do, but I appreciate it more than I have a problem with it. It is a symbol of our kindness.

I do hate it immensely when we are seen as living, breathing ATMs. Sometimes I feel kak because some people take advantage of this kindness and ask you for money for beer and cigarettes – these are not real needs, they are vices. If you choose a vice you should pay for it yourself. But, hey, ask me for a drink anytime. If I can get it for you I will, because I was also taught how to give without feeling bitter about it.

When someone asks me for money for something as basic as food, I never object. I feel a certain level of guilt and simply give them money, even if my petrol tank is on reserve. At least I know that when I get home, I have food in my fridge and I would also have made a difference in someone's life, even if only for that moment, if only for that day.

This is the kind of blessing and ubuntu that we did not know we were being taught when we were young. But it's there and alive, and yes, it's a black thing.

PRIMROSE MRWEBI has directed and performed in poetry productions, facilitated writing workshops at different festivals and been a guest teacher at writing centres. She has written for publications like *Cosmopolitan*, *Fairlady* and *Bona* and works as an MC at literary events. Primrose was a featured poet at the opening of Parliament in 2004. Her children's book for isiXhosa and English learners will be published soon. She also runs a literacy programme in Khayelitsha.

The circle will not be unbound

Bongani Kona

1.

Lately, I have been thinking of *Death of a Salesman* – Arthur Miller's rebuke of the 'winner takes all' rat race that is the American Dream. I was 15 when I first read the play for a high school class. The central character, a working-class man named Willy Loman, takes his own life at the end of it; the tragic dénouement of a crisis precipitated by his retrenchment.

'I don't say he's a great man,' Linda, his wife, says in the eulogy delivered in the final act. 'Willie Loman never made a lot of money. His name was never in the paper. He's not the finest character that ever lived. But he's a human being, and a terrible thing is happening to him. So attention must be paid. He's not to be allowed to fall into his grave like an old dog. Attention, attention must be finally paid to such a person.'[1]

I've never forgotten those lines.

Why begin by telling you all this? Because I don't have a proper grasp of economics or the mechanisms underpinning the vast financial universe we live in. I am a reader. Which is to say that my understanding of the world – and by 'understanding' I mean how to live morally – has been shaped by words. Stories. Stories written and shared with me by others.

You ask me to tell you about 'black tax' and I can respond the only way I know how. By telling stories.

It begins like this.

Two summers ago, my mother, then 70 years old, had a dream that foreshadowed a season of illness. When she told me about the dream the following morning, she said she had seen a ghostly apparition angling towards her. Suddenly, the room felt cold and she couldn't breathe.

'I thought I was a goner,' she said, moving her head sideways.

How had I known to visit that morning, as my mother sat in her night clothes, still shaken by the dream? *La sangre llama*, the Spanish saying goes. Blood calls. Blood calls to blood.

This, then, is a story of blood, of kin. Our calling out to one another. If you play the tape in reverse, to the question, 'Are you with us?' the poet Ed Pavlić says, you'll hear the hidden message underlined: 'Are we within you?' Likewise, the students of Black Study argue that 'being black is a thing you can only do with others. I don't know that it's possible to be black by oneself.'[2] Neither, I might add, is it desirable.

This sociality, our being together, is what we imprecisely call 'black tax'. Imprecise because it frames as a burden our ways of preserving life in the face of forces mobilised against it. So as not to fall into our graves like old dogs.

I was abandoned by my father at birth and, for years afterwards, I dreamt that he walked the streets looking for me. Seeking me out. His own flesh and blood, as the old saying goes. But he did not. And like so many other black men I know, I am here largely because of the women in my family. The constellation of aunts, sisters, cousins, mother, grandmother, etc, who stood between me and the world.

But this is not one of those clichés about the strength of black women. Still, I should mention that statistically, black women earn less than men in the workplace. And yet, despite those odds, or because of them, the women in my family taught me that love is work. And that work – that love, the collective capacity to care for one another – is what overcomes capital in the end.

'The overcoming of capital has to be fundamentally based on the simple insight,' the cultural theorist Mark Fisher wrote in the introduction to his unpublished manuscript *Acid Communism*, 'that, far from being about wealth creation, capital necessarily and always blocks the production of common wealth.'[3] It erodes the bonds between you and me, dear reader.

2.

I am the third and last of my mother's blood children. My sister Caroline and my brother J. are 16 and 14 years older than me, respectively. I grew up in Hatfield, a lower-middle-class neighbhourhood in the south of Harare, and in the spring of 1992, my mother moved to Cape Town on the back of a job offer from a university there.

By that time, J. and Caroline were fully grown and making their way in the world. I stayed behind with my grandmother, Agnes, who earned a pension and made dresses in her spare time, Aunt Sheila, a receptionist at the public examinations board, her son Themba, who is only five months older than me, and Uncle Ed, then employed by a parastatal in a small town 73 kilometres west of Harare. He lived there during the week, returning on weekends.

If it takes a village to raise a child, then this was mine. But it was a village whose population was always in flux. Other relatives constantly moved in and out of the house in Hatfield. A cousin would arrive to take up study at the polytechnic or at the university. An aunt would stop by for a night en route to a church conference. And so it went.

My mother's departure, however, remains the single most heart-breaking episode of my childhood. The kind of hurt that sits in the bone, like sediment at the base of a river. I replayed the scene over and over again in my head: standing on the stoep that sun-drenched afternoon, waving goodbye to her as she sat in the back seat of a Rixi Taxi racing towards the airport.

Why had she left? Why hadn't she taken me with her? Days afterwards, I remember lips curling downwards and bursting into tears in class after the teacher asked us to write a composition on the subject, 'My Family'.

Her absence filled the world.[4]

It felt like I'd lost another parent, but my mother's going away opened up possibilities for us that were sealed off before. My family didn't own a car – that prime symbol of upward mobility – and yet, Themba and I attended the best government school in the country. A decision that would shape the trajectory of our futures. My mother would visit three times a year and she would call every Sunday. Even now, 26 years later, as I sit here telling you this story, she still picks up the telephone every Sunday and smiles into the static.

But until I left the country myself, aged 18, enfolding my grandmother in my arms as we said goodbye, I didn't understand the logic behind the choices my mother had made. She hadn't left because of me. She left *for* me. For us. And that's a different story.

To be an immigrant, after all, is to shoulder the hopes and dreams of others. Sometimes those dreams are small. 'Mama, ndicela undithengele iballoon e-red' – Mama, please buy me a red balloon – a boy says, whispering into the telephone. But at other times, those hopes are heavier: school fees, house renovations, medical treatments, a death in the family.

Love is work. And sometimes, that work is hard.

3.

Here's another story: in a 2013 interview with the South African short story writer Stacy Hardy, published in *Chimurenga*, Pakistani novelist Mohsin Hamid is quoted as saying, 'No self-help book can be complete without taking into account our relationship with the state.' Neither, I suppose, would any discussion on overcoming capital. States govern how we live. 'States tug at us. States bend us. And tirelessly, states seek to determine our orbits.'[5]

In the late 1990s, beset by political unrest at home and embroiled in a costly war in the Democratic Republic of Congo, the Zimbabwean economy began to unravel. Gradually at first, then gathering pace until prices rose by the hour. In 2008, inflation stood at a staggering 79 600 000 000 per cent and unemployment somewhere in the eightieth percentile.

My grandmother lost her pension and no matter how hard Aunt Sheila and Uncle Edwin worked, they would never have money left over at the end of the week, let alone the end of the month. In less than ten years, seemingly overnight if you consider the *longue durée* of history, a whole country was plunged into destitution.

Millions fled. And before the Home Office in the United Kingdom took the step of introducing visa requirements for Zimbabweans travelling to Britain in 2002, the earliest wave of migration headed in that direction.

'I have decided to bring in a visa programme for Zimbabwe to deal with what is very significant abuse of our immigration controls by Zimbabwean nationals,'[6] Mr David Blunkett, then Home Secretary, smugly told a reporter for *The Guardian* newspaper in response to the rising numbers. What do the former colonial powers owe the world? How much should they be taxed? But those are questions for another time.

Inevitably, this labour migration would turn towards South Africa. All our hopes lay there. I'm trying to tell you now the collective story of what coming to this country symbolised to those of us who live here. It represented a chance to *literally* earn a living.

In the vacuum created by the breakdown of the Zimbabwean state, families depend on remittances sent back home. According to a 2017 study by the Zimbabwe National Statistics Agency, more than 50 per cent of Zimbabweans living here had sent money home in the previous year.[7] When, recently, I asked my mother about this – she's retired now – she said she would send as much as half her salary back home to us.

4.

In Samanta Schweblin's hallucinatory debut novel, *Fever Dream*, a young mother describes the instinctive connection to her daughter as being governed by a 'rescue distance' – 'the invisible thread that ties us together.'[8] A thread that tightens or unspools depending on gut feeling.

Two summers ago, when my mother had the dream I've already told you about, I lived alone in a small garden flat in Cape Town, three kilometres away from her. I'm neither rich nor poor but I'd managed to build a life on the back of the many sacrifices she had made. And so that morning, as we sat together in her two-bedroomed apartment, light filtering in through the gauze curtains, her face drained of colour, I instinctively felt the rescue distance tightening.

'My appetite,' she said, poking around the egg I'd put on her plate with a fork, 'I don't seem to have any appetite.'

By that week's end, she could no longer walk 20 metres without running short of breath and she was disorientated. Like my grandmother, Agnes, my mother is someone whom you might call a big reader. That she now couldn't read, the letters dancing off the page, was a bad omen.

I moved back in with her and we drove to a local GP to run some tests. Then, more tests. On Friday afternoon, the GP, a tall white man with wispy grey hair and clear blue eyes who spoke in a soft-grained monotone, called to say the results had come from the lab and we needed to come to his office as soon as possible.

We drove down Rondebosch Main Road in silence. A silence laden with all sorts of questions and fears. It's never a good sign when the doctor summons you to his office. *Kidneys*, he said. *Something, something. Water-electrolyte imbalance. Specialists. Something, something. More tests.* The words kept jumping at us.

The following morning, at dawn, we drove to Groote Schuur, the teaching hospital situated on the slopes of Devil's Peak. My mother was admitted and she remained in hospital for close to a fortnight, and for the time that she was there, undergoing a battery of tests, ultra-sounds, X-rays, etc, I went to see her in the afternoon, from 3 pm to 4 pm, and lingered in the hallways until the evening visiting hours, 7 pm to 8 pm.

I met so many people in those two weeks, people whose names I now can't recall. Others who lost loved ones. But, perhaps, our names really didn't matter. Everything we needed to know about each other was written on the surface. Every conceivable emotion collected on our faces.

If you tipped your head to the ceiling, you could see the invisible threads of hope we were each holding on to, and by the simplest of gestures – a quick sideways glance, say, or the gentle brush of hands as you crossed each other in the corridors – you were drawn into a world of sadness, fear, worry or despair. We knew the weight of each other's stories and because of that we held each other with kindness. It was our duty to do so.

I'm coming, now, to the hardest part of the story. My mother was diagnosed with end-stage renal failure. At 70, the doctors said, it would be too risky for her to undergo a transplant and besides, the waiting list was long, with preference given to younger patients.

The only other option would be haemodialysis. How it works is, because your kidneys can no longer filter waste and regulate water and acid in the blood, the blood is put through a filter outside your body, cleaned, and then returned into your body. This is done, on average, three times a week. The problem was that at over sixty, my mother no longer qualified for state-funded dialysis treatment and without it, she would be dead within days.

The palliative care specialist I spoke with had advised that since treatment can exceed R3 000 a week, the kindest thing to do for people without adequate medical cover would be to let the story come to an end.

'We call this comfort care,' she said. Besides, unlike cancer, death from end-stage kidney failure is relatively painless, she added, but not in those words.

As a boy, speaking on the telephone with my mother, I'd never imagined that I would one day sit here and be asked to put a price on her life. To measure its worth in rands and cents. This woman had given everything to me and yet, I knew if it came down to it, I couldn't save her. Not by myself I couldn't. And if it hadn't been for my brother J., this story would have had a different ending. But we chose life. Whatever the cost, we chose life.

5.

Have you heard the story about elephants, how their lives move in a circle? But before I tell you that story, you should know that I cancelled my lease and moved back in with my mother. She had always looked after me, but now our roles have been reversed. She started reading again, and every two weeks or so, I get a stack of books from the library. How does the old expression go? We've come full circle.

Until she made the switch to peritoneal dialysis, which you can self-administer at home, my mother had to undergo haemodialysis treatment at a private medical facility in Observatory. We woke up at 4 am, 3 days a week – Monday, Wednesday and Friday – in order to be at the hospital by 5 am. She would stay there until ten in the morning, but I would be home by 5:30 am, getting ready for work. I wouldn't say that all of this was easy. By the end of the day I would be tired to the bone.

But love is work. And sometimes, that work is hard.

So, the elephants. The story goes that when the elephant senses that she's near the end of the circle of life, she'll leave the herd behind. But not on her own. She'll pick a companion – a friend, sister, relative – and together they'll walk for days, sometimes even weeks, across the savannah. Until, finally, the dying elephant picks a spot she deems suitable as a final resting place. She'll mark this place, which the companion is not allowed to enter, by tracing a circle. Then, finally, she'll say to her companion, goodbye friend and thank you very much for taking me this far. Your time has come to return to the herd. The circle must not be broken.[9]

I like this story because it's really about life. Sometimes, we're called on to accompany the one who is dying and we don't know how close they are to that circle we're not allowed to enter and we don't know when we'll be told to turn back. And because life is circular, someday it will be you and I selecting a companion to travel with us.

What I'm tell you is that what you call 'black tax' is what we call life. And the circle will not be unbound.

BONGANI KONA is a writer and contributing editor at *Chimurenga*. His writing has appeared in *Safe House: Explorations in Creative Non-fiction* and *Prufrock*, on BBC Radio 4 and in a variety of other publications and anthologies. He was shortlisted for the 2016 Caine Prize for African Writing and he is the co-editor of *Migrations* (2017), an anthology of short stories.

Notes

1 Miller, A. *Death of a Salesman*. 1949. New York: Viking Press.
2 Eshun, K. Inaugural Mark Fisher Memorial Lecture delivered at Goldsmiths, University of London, 19 January 2018.
3 Fisher, M. *Acid Communism*, quoted by Kodwo Eshun during the inaugural Mark Fisher Memorial Lecture delivered at Goldsmiths, University of London, 19 January 2018.
4 The title of an artwork by William Kentridge.
5 Mohsin Hamid interviewed by Stacy Hardy in *Chimurenga Chronic,* August 2013.
6 Travis, A. 'Zimbabweans must get visas to enter UK', in *The Guardian*, 7 November 2002.
7 2017 Survey by the Zimbabwe National Statistics Agency, published in *NewsDay* (Zimbabwe), 22 January 2018.
8 Schweblin, S. *Fever Dream* translated by Megan McDowell. 2017. New York: Riverhead Books.
9 This story is adapted from 'Tracing a Circle' by Antonio Tabucchi, Translated by Elizabeth Harris, in *PEN America: A Journal for Writers and Readers*. Issue #17

PART 4

Casting a spell on poverty

Nkateko Masinga

It's a story you will read on the front page of every South African newspaper in the first week of the year: from the dusty streets of – insert relevant village/township/squatter camp: a young star has beaten the odds and passed the Grade 12 examinations with 'flying colours' (code for admission to pursue a bachelor's degree with a bagful of distinctions).

The odds that have been beaten can include – but are not limited to – dire poverty, a child-headed household due to abandonment or the death of one or both parents, demotivated and/or absent teachers and under-resourced schools. It's the numerous things we cannot bear to name because we are ashamed that we have to watch wordlessly as young people wrestle with them for 12 years, knowing that only some will succeed in the end.

We wait, with bated breath and applause held, for the moments when the Goliath of failure hits the ground. Then we heave a collective, rehearsed sigh of relief and lift our newest young champion in the air.

These against-all-odds stories are so addictive that South Africans have begun to romanticise the struggles that young, mostly black, learners, must endure to be granted access to institutions of higher learning. I call it poverty porn. It represents the unwavering belief that from dust comes achievement, that those who fail have no excuse for doing so: *if so-and-so could produce such amazing results coming from this area, what is stopping you?*

Each time the charade that is the Grade 12 exam results announcement takes place, I ask myself if any measures have been put in place to ensure more support for new university students with this kind of background. The answer, of course, is no. I also wonder what type of career guidance these learners have access to.

In my time – my Grade 11 and 12 years were in 2008 and 2009 – we would circulate a list of the highest-paying jobs in the country and then find out which university qualifications we needed in order to qualify for those jobs. We wanted money, plain and simple. Thoughts of taking gap years and sabbaticals or pursuing passions were reserved for the privileged.

In 'How "black tax" cripples our youth's aspirations' (*Mail & Guardian*, 15 October 2015) Mosibudi Ratlebjane interviewed young South Africans who are buckling under the pressure of being the family breadwinners. She describes black tax as 'the extra money that black professionals are coughing up every month to support their extended families' and very aptly also as a 'regular tithe'. The comparison between tithing at church and giving money to one's family is fitting because this is an almost religious activity; a commitment made from both responsibility and guilt.

In my fourth year of university, a deacon at my church in Mamelodi told me that the entire congregation was waiting for my monthly tithe. It had already been decided, long before, that ten per cent of my earnings every month would be going to the church. The thought made me very anxious.

In my first year of medical school, I continued to live with my parents and used taxis and City of Tshwane buses to get to university every day. Morning traffic, coupled with taxi strikes and the overall unreliability of public transport in South Africa, meant that I was often late for my first lecture.

When we started doing practicals, which sometimes required us to be on campus as early as 6 am, I told my parents I needed to either move closer to campus or get a car. They were sympathetic but explained that they could not afford to buy me a car or pay for me to stay at a university residence or private accommodation close to campus. Luckily, my fees were paid in full by an academic merit award I had received from the university. I had to resign myself to the fact that the accommodation issue would have to wait.

However, my constant latecoming began to reflect in the results of my class assessments, which worried me. My first thought was to look for a part-time job, an idea I was talked out of by friends who had attempted it and failed. My next thought was to secure funding through a bursary or scholarship. This took me to the 1 Military Hospital, in Thaba Tshwane; a friend, who had a military bursary, said that it was an easy process 'if you knew people'. He took me there and said he would put in a word for me if necessary. I waited for months but never heard back from them and started looking at other options.

Towards the end of my first year, application forms for Department of Health bursaries came out and I submitted mine, heavy with hope. My acceptance letter came that December, and thus my second year in medical school began with my financial woes eased. With this bursary, I had enough funds for my tuition, accommodation, food and textbooks.

When I started living on my own for the first time that year, I learnt that for black university students, black tax is not something you start paying when you have completed your degree and gotten a job. Even if you are the recipient of a bursary or loan, a significant portion of your stipend must be sent home so that you can help the family with living expenses. I had friends who were living on noodles and refrigerated bread, but were content in the knowledge that back home, all was well.

My friends and I used to daydream about our first pay cheques. While we walked from one class to the next, we would talk about the things we would be able to buy once we started working. Some spoke of putting down a deposit on their first car, others of saving for a trip abroad. We all mentioned our families: how we would pay for our siblings' school fees, fix the gate at home, buy dad a new car.

University was a strange environment. White students bought expensive wraps and tramezzinis at the school cafeteria daily and drove onto campus in cars similar to those of our professors. Even those who lived on campus had cars and drove out on weekends to see their families and friends.

Our worlds did not merge, not even in lecture halls. The unspoken rule was that you sat with people who looked like you. To be a black student with white friends required that you ate what they ate and drove what they drove.

However, the contact with white students in class could help you gain access to some of the things race had deprived you of. The thing is, white students had access to past papers and the legendary 'question bank', a digital file that had thousands of questions and answers that came up in computer-generated tests. If your black classmate with a private school education and class privilege could get access to the question bank, his job was to send the ladder back down for you and the rest of the black students.

It seems the against-all-odds stories continue until we die.

Those who make it, after years of struggling – often both academically and financially, sleeping in the university's study labs and toilets because on-campus accommodation is too costly and unfairly distributed – finally get to wear their black wizard cloaks.

You see, black students and black graduates are like magicians. Firstly, with their bursaries and then with their salaries, they must cast spells to rescue their families from poverty. Their degree supposedly confers on them the ability to make a car, a house and a new life materialise. As if by magic.

The moment you leave university, with the spell-book, there is an important spell you need to cast immediately: the spell to reverse poverty by paying black tax. This is how it is cast: a black student's monthly stipend must be sent home. There are many expenses to consider. The roof is leaking and must be fixed, Mama's stokvel account is overdue, younger sis wants to go on a school excursion and needs money for the trip and food, uncle so-and-so is in hospital.

For students who are living away from home, every telephonic conversation with relatives must include the line, 'Don't worry, when I start working, I will be able to do more.'

The black graduate's first pay cheque belongs to their family. There are many debts to repay. The uncle whose computer was used to fill in the application form for admission, the neighbour who gave the graduate – then still a high-schooler – taxi fare to attend the university's open day. Many went to bed hungry to send the graduate to school and all those who contributed to his or her success must be compensated when the graduate is able to assist.

Nothing says, 'I am in a position to assist,' like the first pay cheque. It doesn't even matter how much the black graduate earns. All that matters is that money is coming in and poverty is on its way out.

However, reversing poverty to the point of invisibility occurs in two stages. The first stage is when those monitoring the life of the young black professional begin to see that he or she has started making money; this may be through the flaunting of a flashy sports car or a new penchant for expensive brand-name clothing and fine dining. Stage two is when the family of the young black professional benefits from the money that is coming in.

You see, for those watching the family of the graduate, it is a disgrace for a black professional to buy things for themselves and neglect those left behind. It is not uncommon to hear that 'so-and-so has forgotten that he was raised on these very streets, he now drives his fancy car and does not give his mother a cent.'

It takes more than this spell to get rid of the beast of poverty, but you must do it because in the eyes of the community, no one is successful until their entire family is successful. In Trevor Noah's bestselling memoir, *Born a Crime*, he quotes his mother referring to 'the black tax' and saying, 'Because the generations who came before you have been pillaged, rather than being free to use your skills and education to move forward, you lose everything just trying to bring everyone behind you back up from zero.'

I often say, half-jokingly, that if someone had taken me to a hospital to shadow a doctor while I was in high school, I probably would not have wanted to go to medical school. The reality is that many students enter the gates of a university knowing very little about the career that their chosen university programme will lead them to. This takes me to a part of my own story that I hardly ever tell, but probably should.

In conversation, even in interviews, I have told the embellished version – where I decided to pursue a degree in medicine because I was an ill child, who was in and out of hospital because of childhood asthma. I have also shared a version of the story where someone told me to 'pay it forward if you can't pay it back' – without mentioning that this person was a fellow patient in a psychiatric facility – and how these words prompted me to consider a career as a medical doctor and, perhaps, as a paediatric psychiatrist. I am certain it was marked as a delusion of grandeur in my records, that I, a patient in a psych ward, talked about wanting to become a psychiatrist.

When I was in Grade 11, I told my parents I wanted to study creative writing. I had just started in a new school because, at the age of 15, I was diagnosed with clinical depression and struggling to cope at school. The new school was smaller and more academically inclined. At my old school, I had been mocked for being a top academic achiever. I was called ugly, my skirt was too long and I did not qualify to be part of the popular crowd. I realise, now, that I was a victim of bullying. At my new school, though, my intelligence was celebrated over my appearance and I began to thrive.

In 2009, my Grade 12 English teacher, Mrs De Bruin, told me she could picture me as a newsreader or television broadcaster. She told me I spoke 'the Queen's English' – which is, of course, the result of British colonialism, but it pleased me to hear this nonetheless. While reading a brochure I had taken at the University of Pretoria's open day earlier that year, my eyes lingered on the page with qualifications in the Faculty of Humanities. It was love at first sight.

Days after receiving the brochure, I was deciding between a Bachelor of Arts (BA) degree in English Literature or a BA in Journalism. The latter appealed to me because there seemed to be jobs in journalism and I would have one: I could write for newspapers and magazines; I could read the news or be a field reporter.

But first, I needed to sell the dream to my family. I remember the day I requested a family meeting to discuss my future. There was an air of seriousness in the room. There we sat, my parents and I, at the dinner table, talking about journalism and English literature as possible career options. My parents were not pleased with my plans. My mother felt that I would be wasting my time and would not find a job.

For several days after this, she would taunt me as we watched the news.

She would point at field reporters on the TV screen and ask condescendingly, 'Is that what you want to do, run around in the blistering heat all day, asking cabinet ministers for a comment?'

I was defeated, embarrassed. I already knew I would have to pay for my own studies and it seemed unlikely that I would find a sponsor for a BA degree. My parents told me if I could find a bursary or scholarship that would fund my chosen degree, they would reconsider their decision and allow me to do what I wanted.

I remember scouring the internet and newspapers looking for bursaries and seeing one that said BEng. For a moment, I was elated. A while later, I realised it was a qualification in engineering, not English. I was crushed. It was clear that if I wanted a stress-free transition to university life, I needed to study something in the area known as STEM: science, technology, engineering and mathematics.

The friends I spoke to about my predicament said it would be a waste of my mathematics and physical sciences results to pursue anything besides a health sciences degree. It made sense. It kept me up many nights, but I decided they were right. After all, I had chosen maths and science in Grade 10 because they were a gateway to high-paying jobs.

When I remembered the mission, I gave up the idea of a BA and started analysing a different page in the University of Pretoria's brochure: I diverted my attention to the Faculty of Health Sciences. The following year, I became the head girl at my new school and the news began to spread: Nkateko was going to be a doctor. I was joining the club of people who could someday afford to go on vacation and buy new houses for their mothers.

I took on the dream of being a future doctor with gusto. I

wore the title proudly. In 2009, I finished Grade 12 with five distinctions and provisional acceptance into medical school. Medicine being the competitive programme that it is, I was going up against students from all over the country with a so-called full house (seven to ten distinctions). I was accepted into my second-choice course, BSc Biological Sciences, with the exciting option to take Bachelor of Medicine and Bachelor of Surgery (MBChB) subjects in the first semester of my first year and then apply to transfer to medicine.

My dreams of being a writer seemingly abandoned, I took on the challenge and by 2010 I was admitted to the University of Pretoria's Faculty of Health Sciences. The following year, I received a letter saying that I had been admitted into the Golden Key International Honour Society, as I was in the top 15 per cent of my class academically. I was in my element, it seemed.

I enjoyed the first three years of medical school. The coursework was challenging but manageable and I still found time to write and occasionally perform at poetry 'open mic' events. In fourth year, the beginning of full-time clinical rotations and oral examinations, my enthusiasm for the course dwindled. In that year, we began rotating through the various specialities of medicine in preparation for the student internship complex: a vigorous 18-month long, in-hospital training programme from the middle of fifth year to the end of sixth year.

My health also began to suffer.

Precautions are taken to keep medical students healthy during the course of their studies: they are subjected to compulsory hepatitis B vaccines and boosters, 'starter-packs' with a first dose of post-exposure prophylactic antiretroviral therapy medication in the event of a needle prick-injury, gloves and masks. I was aware of the various occupational hazards that came with being a health professional, but nothing could have prepared me for the toll it would take on my own health.

The worst of my bouts of illness came in fifth year when I contracted pneumonia from one of my patients in the paediatric ward. I took a course of antibiotics and recovered after several weeks, but this incident left me jaded. I decided that I was going to push through until the end of the course but there was no way I was going to practise if my life was as risk.

I left medicine for good at the end of my sixth year. I am now a full-time writer and I feel lucky to be able to do what I love. There are times when I wish I had followed my heart from the beginning and pursued a qualification in literature. At other times, I wish I had followed through on my medical studies and completed my internship and community service. This thought usually occurs to me when people from the church I no longer attend ask what I am doing with my life and my parents tell them that I am doing nothing.

I run a small publishing firm to supplement my income from freelance writing, but this is not something I can tell the deacon, who expects that a tithe of thousands of rands should enter the church's bank account in my name. Fortunately, the requirement to pay ten per cent of my earnings to the church is a type of bondage I have freed myself from and I am content to let the church folk talk.

My parents also struggle to understand. To them, it is easier to believe that I am doing nothing since I haven't given them something to boast about on Sundays.

Years after my dream of studying journalism had been laid to rest, I was interviewed on eNews Channel Africa (eNCA) in connection with an event I was participating in, called '67 Poems for Mandela Day'. I remembered Mrs De Bruin's words and so I sent her a YouTube link to the interview a few days later, with a note saying, 'I see what you meant. You knew all along that I would love this.'

My relationship with my family will continue to be difficult because I am yet to meet their expectations. Not long ago, my father asked me to pay back the money he contributed towards my university studies. I gasped, almost pointing out that in my first year, my fees were paid in full thanks to the academic merit award I had received from the university.

From my second year onwards, it was the Department of Health bursary that covered my tuition. I held my tongue. I know that what he really meant to say is, *I expected more from you.* He's right. I owe him bragging rights within the community. I owe him a fancy German car parked in the yard, so the neighbours know we've made it. I have failed him.

The expectations of black parents and their need to live a life that looks good to others also creates an emotional tax on black professionals. The guilt that I feel for opting out of being their golden child, the family dokotela, gnaws at me at the worst of times. Still, I am quickly consoled by the fact that I am doing what I love instead of what is expected of me.

There are talks of my younger sister, now fifteen, becoming a neuropsychiatrist in future. Perhaps, through her, there is hope for us yet.

NKATEKO MASINGA is a South African poet and 2019 fellow of the Ebedi International Writers Residency. She was nominated for a Pushcart Prize in 2018 and her work has received support from Pro Helvetia, the Liaison Office of the Swiss Arts Council in Johannesburg. She is the contributing interviewer for poetry at *Africa In Dialogue*, an online interview magazine that archives creative and critical insights with Africa's leading storytellers.

Hypothetically peaking

Chwayita Ngamlana

Let us suppose, for a moment, that you are a 'platinum child'. You are born into a stable, middle-class family, your parents are a happily married, black, Xhosa couple in a small, still, scenic town. Let us suppose that from your conception, your parents make it their goal to teach you how to be more than just a human being.

Pumped with classical music, minerals and vitamins, you are ejected from the womb after nine months. You come out looking like the elusive African black diamond and weighing as much as a sack of beetroot, as a healthy baby should, all chubby and well-nourished. The vitamins seem to have preserved and protected you – you are smart and know not to cry unnecessarily.

Once out, you get five-star service; you get the best clothes, food, comfort and entertainment. You are a blessing – a gem – the answer to all rain dances and sacrificial goats. Your parents decide to equip you with the skills of a soldier, a scientist or perhaps a cyborg – part man, part all-government-secrets-and-codes. You represent faith and hope – you are already a dream doll.

At the age of two, you are taken to a crèche where you start learning about colours, shapes, numbers and the sounds of things. Most importantly, you learn how embarrassing it is to wet yourself on your designated green mat during nap time. You also learn about social interaction. For instance, boys are different, they are annoying and they are everywhere, and why does it feel like every girl 'low-key' does not like being around any other girl?

After a few years, you are ready to go to preschool. You are taken to a private preparatory school where you learn true elitism. You no longer have to deal with snotty hands touching you, because this group know how to wipe their noses. You also do not need to carry lunch to school because everyone gets a cooked meal during and after school. You learn how to run away from boys every day because they are constantly trying to play catch-and-kiss. You play hide-and-seek so you can develop the skill of being incognito when need be.

Puzzles and the sizes of things start being important, that and English. The birthday parties have themes and costumes and the birthday cakes are in the shape of Superman's coat or Barbie's ball gown. The parties are held in big backyards where there are dogs and a pool. You are used to seeing three two-litre fizzy drinks and a plate or two of potato chips placed in the centre of a random steel table. This is new.

At the age of seven, you start Grade 1 at a private school. You are a *big* girl. You are still learning more about privilege and your existence is starting to matter more and more each day. More English words are learnt, a word or two of Afrikaans is introduced and along with all of that, a music instrument or two are now accessible.

After the second grade, however, you are taken out of the

private primary school to a public school where you start your third grade. The intricacies of this shift are not fully explained to you, but you go along with it. The transition goes well – you are skipping rope, being freer and more expressive during break times. The only difference is that there are no longer any cooked meals. The focus slowly veers away from privilege and access: now you have to prove yourself in the classroom, somehow.

From Grades 4 to 6, you start realising that you are quite good at writing essays. You are killing English and all that comes with it. You are great at analysing novels like *The Lord of the Flies*. You are also a beast at mathematics and you play the recorder very well. You are showing a lot of promise. For a black girl, you are a genius.

In Grade 7, you are told that you run the world. In your all-girls school, a lot of value is placed on intelligent, active young women. You have PT (physical training) lessons where you learn how to swim and be competitive. When the teachers are not looking, you learn how to deal with bullying. You also get better and better at communicating effectively.

This is also the time you realise you have become too old for certain things; it is no longer cool to be jumping or skipping around on the school playground. Now, you hear people talk about the 'social' last weekend: who made out with whom, who wants whom, and who danced with whom from our brother school. You do not understand much about all of that – boys – yet and so you invest your time in being emotionally available for your best friend who is going through things at home that you never thought were real. Big words, like 'abuse', start to creep into your vocabulary.

You also learn a little more about entrepreneurship as you sell small bags of crushed chocolate for 50 cents each. It becomes a lucrative business – you are sold out every day. The future looks promising, you are a good saleswoman. Apart from English, you realise that you really like music and mathematics.

When you graduate to high school – Grade 8 is quite a trip – you learn to do things you do not necessarily want to do like three-hour examinations and oral presentations. The orals are everywhere, in every subject. Sometimes you are prepared, other times you wing it and fail. Orals are intended to teach you how to assert yourself and develop a likeable personality – these qualities will supposedly take you far in life.

You also start to learn the importance of group work: you hate it, but in the real world, you will have to take part in it; to be adaptable is an asset.

Love-wise, you are also quickly introduced to the term 'cheating' when your supposed boyfriend from the brother school hits on a classmate after only two weeks of dating, and practically ignores you. It is crushing but the lesson to be learnt is that your personal life should never affect your grades. You are a warrior, a phoenix and still the platinum, cyborg, diamond child.

At home, you are still being preserved and sheltered. You are a high commodity now – an investment. You are not allowed to go out at night and you are barely allowed to go to school socials – no boy is going to come and get you pregnant, nothing is going to ruin your future.

In Grade 10, you start crushing on a boy in your brother school who your friends think is ugly. Somehow, your heart jumps when you see him, he is part of the cool crew. You keep looking at each other at joint choir events.

Out of the blue, you hear that his friend wants you instead. The friend is rich but unattractive. Now you learn the importance of money and status. So, you share a kiss with this young man that you do not like, your first and most disgusting kiss.

'Just stick it out, he will buy you things!' your friends say. However, he can sense the lack of authenticity and he ends up looking elsewhere. What have you learnt?

1. You are a bad actress.
2. You are no longer a saleswoman; you are unable to finesse.

In Grade 11, you are showing a lot more promise than before. You are respected and assigned certain leadership roles by the school. You choose to do all your subjects on higher grade because your father told you that you could do it. Your parents want you to optimise your intelligence, that high IQ you were born with . . . apparently.

The future is still bright even though you are piss-poor at science – both physics and chemistry – but hey, you are still killing the English essays and you do the most comical Afrikaans group orals. Higher grade maths is a huge challenge now, but you take it in your stride and take advantage of your father's mathematical genius.

You start doing aerobics because a female's looks are something that needs to be nurtured and maintained. They say you have to participate in sport and extra-mural activities for a certain number of hours a week, so your parents buy you a squash racket and a tennis racket. Then there's your dedicated participation in the school choir. *These are the makings of a*

Boss Bitch, you think to yourself . . . because now, you also know colourful language.

In Grade 12, the school makes you one of only 15 prefects. You are also among the five leaders in the choir committee and you are appointed deputy chairperson of the Interact Club. As a prefect, it is your responsibility to monitor people during break-times and to make sure that everyone speaks only English in the corridors.

They give you the task of preserving and uplifting the school spirit, so you design an award system for the school. During assembly, these A5 certificates are given to learners who achieved something in the last week or two. The point is to encourage them to keep doing well. The teachers embrace the concept, and the learners are happy to be acknowledged in front of the whole school.

You start to learn the importance of inclusion and you are developing as a public speaker – something you thought you would never be able to do. You get half-colours for your cultural involvement – something you never thought you would get. Your parents are proud; this is what they paid for, now you are starting to get it.

Your parents keep reminding you how intelligent you are and how happy they are with your progress. During matric, you start applying for university and you choose to study for a Bachelor of Commerce at one of the country's top five universities, with the hope that you will major in marketing and one day become an executive director at an advertising agency.

You pass matric with merit and enrol at university. But shortly after, things start to crumble. The jump from high school to tertiary is vast. You are not getting the hang of accounting or economics and you are failing dismally. It does not help that you are also sexually assaulted in your first year. You start to experience how easily one can become a failure and disappointment to others while also feeling like shit deep within.

At the end of the year, you move to another city and you get accepted to study at a very prestigious university. You are back on track again. Finally, you are doing what you always wanted to do – singing.

But the standards at this institution are even higher and there are many courses and twice as many exams. All those practicals. You are not part of the top five or even the top ten in class. You get passed from vocal teacher to vocal teacher because, apparently, no one can get through to you – you do not put in enough hours and you choose big songs prematurely. You are not necessarily failing but you are averaging at best.

Your friend is getting 80 per cent and above. The man you keep throwing yourself at does not want you. He uses you but, really, does not want you. Things are spiralling out of control, fast. You feel useless, you start sinking. But at home, you are still the platinum dream doll, diamond, cyborg child.

Fast forward a few years into the future: it is even closer – the face of failure. You have developed syndromes and clinical conditions that you never thought you would have to learn to pronounce. You cut your hair. You do not step out of your flat for anything other than junk food and painkillers. You start taking 12 to 20 painkillers a day but they do not heal the anxiety, the emptiness, and this fleshy mess.

You see a psychologist but it is a waste of time and money. You feel guilty for not attending classes and being absent from campus. You also feel guilty for not being good at things that seem basic.

Your parents invested everything in you. Remember, you are carrying their faith, their hope, their future and their dreams. You are one of the few of your generation – on both sides of the family – that have made it this far. But now it is all in vain.

Eventually, you realise that you cannot bounce back on your own, so you accept defeat. You allow the university to call your parents and tell them that you have been diagnosed with depression and your scheduled examinations have all been deferred to give you time to recover.

How did you get here?

You go home and they do not understand. How could you drop the ball so close to victory? The whole family gets involved, everyone has an opinion. You spend months trying to explain something that even you do not understand.

They tell you to go back and try again the following year and so you do. It is no different. You are lost and you are hurting, despite such a solid foundation. You were so carefully put together, nothing was out of place. Somehow, you have managed to unravel yourself. You have gone from being a leader to a being a wanderer, a recluse.

After two years of random odd jobs, you return to your hometown and are luckily accepted into the local university . . . because the race must still be finished. So, you get your shit together and you study all the way up to a master's degree. It seems you are back on track; the family believes in you again. There is a cheer here and a cheer there.

You are sent out into the world to try again, there is no way you will not succeed now. You need to prove to them all that you were worth all the investment.

You try to apply for a degree-appropriate job, but no one believes that someone of your race could legitimately have received that qualification. You hustle; do a short course here and another one there, but the powers that be still do not believe you. Now the issue is your blackness; you could never perform better than a white opponent. You learn that you were never a candidate to begin with. Shortlisting only means they gave you a chance, but whether you killed the interview or not is irrelevant.

You appeal to the black sisters and brothers, with your fist in the air, but they want no part in your hustle. Later, you learn that there is an anxiety that runs deep in the community of black professionals, who constantly fear they will be replaced. You also learn that people love being 'the only black person' in their field, company, department, section, office.

Eventually, your future starts to darken again. It is coming back. Slowly, you return to a different kind of black. You turn to alcohol because the euphoria makes you believe everything is okay. Your parents ask why you have not checked in for a while, and once again you do not know how to explain. Instead, you make grandiose promises and say you have everything under control; a whole chunk of money will come in this time next year, your career is about to take off.

You travel, they invest more without any monetary results, more darkness follows, more emptiness – no one believes you anymore, including the family. So, you cut your hair, for the second time. Cutting your hair is a remodelled way of fasting.

You go home because you can no longer maintain your lifestyle. All you get are odd jobs. The private schools, the killer English essays, the leadership positions, the degrees, the distinctions, the sheltering, the grooming, the privilege, the intelligence, the preparation, the people skills, the aiming high, being a homebody, *none of it worked*!

Your parents watch with suspense but they no longer believe you. Everyone is looking at you like you have lost your mind. Who gets a lifetime head-start and then comes back empty-handed? The crumbs you earn from time to time and throw into the family pot do not make much of a difference. Still, every last crumb will be taken, make no mistake about that. They afford you a knock or two on your bedroom door before your personal space is invaded.

Soon, you are reduced to an adult-mouth eating helpings that have not been earned or contributed towards. Now, the family is not fucking with you, you had better make fetch happen.

The darkness gets darker, your blackness gets blacker, the tax owed gets even bigger. Everyone is tired of you returning empty-handed. Everyone has forgotten your initial success; they have forgotten the promise. You start losing your voice, your opinion matters less and less. Even those who have odder odd jobs than you are now better than you.

For what you cannot contribute financially, you pay with your freedom. You do not deserve respect and space in the family because you have not become an adult yet. You are seen as a grown teenager and a living, breathing nuisance and a burden. You talk last, you are heard last. The platinum child fucked up her life and has been demoted to one of the bronze ornaments in the living room.

So you sit there, trying hard to disappear and yet you are gaining weight, ironically becoming more visible. You sit in your room, you barely come out, you try not to eat and you try not to be too loud. The family still somewhat supports you; they just do not believe you.

Now you are paying all kinds of psychological and emotional tax from which you cannot ever escape. Now you are the equivalent of an ad lib on a rap or kwaito song – totally unnecessary but fun to have around from time to time.

You ask yourself, have you peaked? Is this all you have to offer?

Your inner voices promptly wake up and say in unison, '*Yes . . . yes . . . this is it. You have failed . . . you always fail.*'

CHWAYITA NGAMLANA has a master's degree in creative writing and her debut novel, *If I Stay Right Here*, was longlisted for the Barry Ronge Fiction Prize. Chwayita has been a panellist at prestigious book events such as the Open Book Festival, the South African Book Fair and the Abantu Book Festival. She is currently writing her second novel while working on building a television show, with the likes of Kia Johnson, called *All Woman*.

Beyond the obligation

Lorraine Sithole

This thing people today call black tax has always been such an intimate part of my life that I never even thought of giving it a name. I first heard the term in my MBA class two years ago. A fellow student, a lady, was talking about it with utter disdain and I asked her to explain to me what black tax was. My response afterwards? 'Oh, that sounds like what people do on the daily, there's nothing alarming in that!'

I've had good and bad experiences with black tax. My view on it depends largely on the attitude of the person I'm trying to help. For some, you do it because it's an obligation. For others, like my mother, it goes way beyond an obligation.

Once one of your own children is off the budget, you will gain a niece or nephew who needs to be supported in one way or the other. They might need school transport for a year or further education, even though their parents are both alive and gainfully employed. There can also be a request for accommodation for a niece or nephew who has been accepted into a learnership programme closer to your home than their parents'.

Once, a cousin stayed with me during an internship, but a couple of months into the programme, she quit. She had decided to run her import and export business from our couch! I called my aunt and uncle and sent her home that same afternoon.

The education of my niece came with even more challenges. Since both her parents were still alive and working, I, in my naivety, thought that it was going to be a group effort. I should have braced myself when they wouldn't – or couldn't, the jury is still out on that one – afford to buy her a bus ticket from eThekwini to Johannesburg. So we, my husband and I, had to.

These situations can seem simple when you are on the outside looking in. How hard can it be to put your niece through tertiary education? Well, it quickly becomes much more than a matter of only paying for tuition fees when said niece enrols at an institution hundreds of kilometres from her family home and you still need to look after her daily needs.

Why did she not attend an institution closer to her parents' home, you may ask? Um . . . because she decided very late in the year, after the application window to all government institutions had closed, that she would like to further her studies. She knew her aunty and uncle – my husband and I – valued education more than anything on earth and would do whatever was needed to help.

On arrival, she had a massive toothache and the tooth had to be extracted by a private dentist. Why didn't I send her to our local clinic, I hear you ask? Well, she was in excruciating pain and needed an emergency extraction. Then, after the tooth extraction, there came a series of gynaecological issues which had to be taken care of.

The academic calendar was very close to commencing and

we decided on an institution closer to our home. I used to travel long distances from our home in Protea Glen, in Soweto, to the University of Johannesburg's Auckland Park campus when I was a student and I didn't want my niece to wake up at dawn and negotiate all the challenges associated with using two or three taxis in order to get to classes on time.

Our niece, having everything she needed for the academic year, settled into her studies.

However, as students do, she also made new friends. One became such a good friend that she invited her over for a short stay at our house, but without asking for permission before doing so. We were informed that the friend was visiting for the weekend and when the weekend came and went, there was a lot of ducking and diving.

Eventually, the supposed short visit turned into a three-month stay. At that point we decided it was becoming too costly living with two adult women house guests. We had to take care of food, toiletries *and* their entertainment.

Then there's the parenting and reprimanding you have to do, like waking them up to do chores, because our house is not a hotel. After to-ing and fro-ing with the friend's parents, we had to let her go. What I found astounding was the audacity of her parents, who ducked our calls, as my niece's parents were also doing. This was simply disrespectful. The abdication of their responsibility to their daughter didn't sit well with us.

Today, all the nieces and cousins that have periodically stayed with us have gone back home. One has successfully completed her internship and has secured full-time employment, while another is sitting at home, not making alternative plans like working while studying. But for once, that is not my concern.

My own daughter couldn't finish writing her matric exams due to a breakdown caused by anxiety. She is now my only priority. I will walk with her this year and ensure that she is strong and brave enough to see through her matric exams to the end and look into her future with bright, inspired and empowered eyes.

My mother was an orphan. Well, I guess she is still an orphan, or do you stop being an orphan when you have your own children, I wonder? My mother and her younger sister were raised by a collective of aunts. Aunts who, up to today, still see my mother as their sister's child.

My grandparents – my mother's parents – died when she was a toddler, and she and her younger sister were taken in and looked after by their mother's older sister, Mmamogolo. My mother and her sister, my cherished aunt, did not have much but they had everything they needed to ensure that they became independent black women in apartheid South Africa.

My mother was accepted at Baragwanath Hospital as a student nurse straight after she matriculated. Like today, the government paid students a stipend, which eliminated a lot of bread-and-butter challenges that could otherwise have plagued my mother as a young and poor black female student. My mother used a large percentage of that money to take care of her younger sister and of Mmamogolo, to keep her aunt's household in bread, milk and other staples.

This was simply the way things were done. She had been helped by her aunt and in return she helped Mmamogolo when she was in a position to do so. No questions asked. Therefore, 'black tax' has never been a thing in my life.

My mother has been self-sufficient her whole life. Today, she is in her late sixties and she has always taken care of herself and others. Despite her success in life, she was weighed down by the responsibility of carrying a man who had snatched her dreams and latched onto her like a leech. My father.

When I started working, I carried on living at home with my parents. The plan was to live with them for a year and save up for a down payment towards my first house and also buy a few essentials like a bed, linen, pots, a fridge and maybe a television, before having all the pressures associated with home ownership.

It was very important to me to get a home for myself and my daughter, who was two years old at the time. The sad thing is that I grew up in a home where violence was an everyday language. I would do anything to make sure that my daughter was not constantly exposed to this in the first years of her life.

I had a good job. At the time I was working for a financial institution in an air-conditioned high-rise building, yet my mother did not lay claim to my salary. But still I extended a helping hand because I saw it as an opportunity to alleviate some of the pressure on her. I am my mother's daughter, after all.

I did so by sending a monthly allowance to my elder sister, who was still studying at university. I also bought my younger sister, who was still in high school, toiletries and this and that.

My father, on the other hand, was a different case. He would never ask for anything outright, but should my payday come and go without me giving him cash in hand, he would literally not let anyone sleep. My father thrived on the relative safety and darkness of night. Once a week, he roused the whole house around two o'clock in the morning and went off on a tangent about how I did not respect him in his house.

Somehow, my father, in his twisted mind – for his mind was surely defective – thought that I owed *him* a living – most probably a living wage – for living in their house. I found it so ironic that he believed I had this obligation towards him. After all, it was my mother who had kept us going financially and looked after us.

My mother did not have the opportunity to travel for leisure, neither as a young woman nor as a grown, married one. She never had the opportunity to experience new cultures or create special memories because my father had slowly snuffed out the wonder in her eyes.

For this reason, I decided, three years ago, to take her on a trip to Paris, France. It was the greatest and most special gift I could have bestowed on her. She didn't ask for it. I gifted it to her precisely because she has never asked for that or a double-storey house, nor will she ever ask for anything from her children. I hope to give her many more such opportunities to see the world.

LORRAINE SITHOLE is the founder and president of Bookworms Book Club, which she established in 2011. She is passionate about reading and bringing African authors and stories to the fore. She cooperates with book publishers and retailers to promote books and reading and consults to book fairs and festivals on their literary programmes. Lorraine is currently completing her MBA dissertation on solving distribution challenges faced by niche publishing companies. She also runs a charitable foundation that focuses on increasing access to learning for disadvantaged children.

The hopes and dreams of black parents

Sifiso Mzobe

There is an isiZulu saying that goes, 'Ingane enhle isebenzela ekhaya.' The English translation is, 'A good child works for the household.' And that we do. So well, oh yes, we do.

Why is this, you may ask? Because when you are raised on sacrifice it is only logical (and mostly also a matter of necessity) that you return the favour. The so-called woke amongst us have given it a name – this returning of the favour. They call it black tax. For the purposes of this essay I shall also call it that.

The concept of black tax is drummed into our brains even before we can fully comprehend it. Think of the Christopher Nolan movie *Inception*, and imagine your parents are like the character of Leonardo DiCaprio and his crew, who are trying to infiltrate your subconscious. Their aim, when they get into your subconscious, is to plant an idea. That idea is black tax.

It is important to understand that the life-long attempt at *The Inception of Black Tax* into our subconscious by our parents does not appear out of thin air. It is also not something they come up with while admiring their vast acres of land, while keeping tabs on their investments in the stock exchange or concluding multimillion-rand business deals.

There are several causes of this effect that is black tax – systemic violence, disenfranchisement, poverty, apartheid and a litany of other injustices. Black people have been disenfranchised for too long. It doesn't help that apartheid has morphed from the crude, reprehensible beast of pre-1994 to the slicker, less obvious, but equally damaging economic version of today's rainbow nation.

In the majority of black families, success is a multigenerational quest fuelled by lifelong multigenerational sacrifice. I can recite stories of sacrifice and suffering that will break your heart and at the same time make you applaud the resilience of the black mind. There are so many stories of success against insurmountable odds. Stories that make you realise that if people can make it in life with less than nothing, that means not having enough is not that bad – at least it is something.

This makes it easy to understand why most black parents usher their offspring in the direction of high-paying jobs. Stability is valued above everything else. It is better to have constant and consistent pay because then the money you send back home will be consistent. Avoid at all costs the unpredictable pay of some or other vocation that you choose simply because you have a passion for it. Passion for what? Passion for whom? Passion doesn't pay the bills. Well, not monthly, not consistently, anyway. The pressure on young people to pay black tax is relentless. Now it becomes understandable why it is frowned upon to chase any dreams outside the bracket of stable employment. Chasing your dreams or passion in life is a luxury for the lucky few.

It always boggles the mind when a black household is put under the economic microscope. When the needs of a household are compared to the income of the parents (and at times there is just one parent) you begin to scratch your head. Usually, needs far outweigh income. On top of that, parents still have their own black tax obligations to fulfil to their families. It seems to me that black parents possess a sleight of hand which makes the little income they have go such a long way.

Black parents steer us towards a path of stability. They try to maximise our chances of success and, consequently, the ability to pay black tax. You are not good in mathematics and physics? That doesn't matter. You will still aim to be a doctor, engineer or accountant.

Many young people choose science and maths in high school not because they are good at it, but for the sole reason that *The Inception of Black Tax* has worked on their subconscious. Most of them soon find themselves in limbo when they don't do well in matric. They get sucked into a vicious cycle of matric rewrites and bridging courses.

The Inception of Black Tax is ingrained so deeply in their minds that some people won't consider studying any courses outside the bracket of jobs that will make their parents proud. By the time they realise they are not suited for these subjects, their confidence has been blown to smithereens.

Progress, with regard to economic equality and parity of income, has been slow since 1994. That is the reason why *The Inception of Black Tax* keeps trickling down to every new generation. I have cast many a judgmental side-eye at people who pile pressure on their children at social gatherings. There will always be someone who points to their child and says, 'He will be the first doctor in the family.' Meanwhile, the child is terrible at science but excellent at creative arts.

There are countless other examples of the pressures exerted on young people. 'He will build me a mansion,' 'She will buy me a car,' or 'I put her through school so that she can put her siblings through school,' are some of the comments you often hear. To fail to live up to these dreams is soul-crushing. It is good and necessary to set goals and have dreams for your children, but it is crucial to align their ability to the size of the dream and to try to be objective.

When a black graduate gets a job, they have a lot to make up for compared to their colleagues from better economic backgrounds. They have a deep economic hole to fill before they can start with their own lives. And life is tough in today's economy; sometimes, impossibly tough. Most jobs are in the financial hubs and transport to or accommodation in those hubs is expensive. Young people enter the job market already resigned to a life of credit and debt.

Add to this the customs of culture that we bind ourselves to, which are not at all dynamic and don't adapt with the times. Do you want to get married? Then you must pay for ilobolo and all the many ceremonies that come with it, my friend. And no, the fact that you are going through this process doesn't mean you have been absolved from your black tax obligations. You don't need a calculator to understand that we are talking about major sums of money here.

There is a perfect projection of the life of a black child as imagined by his parent(s) – let's call it the *perfectus trajectoriam*. It goes something like this: black bundle of joy is born; he is handsome, she is pretty.

Black bundle of joy is brilliant in school. Black bundle of

joy attends church religiously. Bundle of joy doesn't smoke or drink alcohol. Bundle of joy passes with flying colours, gets a bursary to study at a prestigious university, aces the degree in record time and becomes a doctor, engineer or accountant.

Bundle of joy immediately finds a high-paying job. If said bundle of joy is male, he will pay the full ilobolo, if she is female, the full ilobolo is paid for her. Bundle of joy marries his or her childhood sweetheart. He/she sends home a constant stream of black tax every month. He/she puts siblings through school and everyone lives happily ever after. If only.

The problem with the *perfectus trajectoriam* is that we assume these two robots – the young man and woman – operate in a vacuum that does not take the realities of life into account. They have no free will and are not at all affected by what goes on around them. How fair are we on our robots if we expect them to see but never be affected by what they see? Children can be shielded as much as possible but life outside the walls always finds a way of worming itself in.

The biggest problem with the *perfectus trajectoriam* is that it leaves absolutely no room for error. Good luck with taking a developing mind and leaving no room for failure. The pressure is immense on these young minds. Parents don't know how to react when they find out that there is a whole lot more that messes with the *perfectus trajectoriam* than there are things supporting it.

In these trying times, confusion sits heavy in the eyes of parents as they watch their children try to navigate this world that is so foreign to them. Perplexed, they see their children try their best to adapt to freelancing, short-term contracts, entrepreneurship and the multiple jobs of today's gig economy. Today's volatile job market is a far cry from the stability that was certain when they were young. The dread in their eyes is absolute when their children try to explain to them that this is the way of the world now.

People passionately put their efforts into business plans or career changes that could be long shots, while worried and confused parents loom in the background. Parents look at their creative daydreamers with immense confusion. They cannot reconcile the reality of the situation with their perfect projections.

They worry about who will carry the financial burden of putting other siblings through school. They vent to their friends. How can this generation diverge so much from the *perfectus trajectoriam*? If only we had the opportunities they have now, they say.

Parents don't understand the world we are living in now. They can't believe their dreams of perfection for their children are not coming true. They are flabbergasted at the thought and sight of the unemployed graduate. They suggest prayer and rituals as a way to summon luck.

But these are different times. Degrees do not guarantee jobs. Our shell-shocked parents simply do not believe that you can struggle to get a job when you have a tertiary qualification. But it happens every day. We often see pictures of frustrated graduates desperate for opportunities. Unemployed graduates resort to standing on street corners with placards detailing their qualifications like street beggars. Engineering graduates begging on the streets for jobs?! Who could have thought? But it happens.

Young, qualified graduates are desperate for an opportunity to play a part in the economy. They are desperate to start their lives, but these are trying times.

Those who manage to stick as closely as possible to the *perfectus trajectoriam* and are fortunate enough to find employment quickly have to contend with stagnation in their own lives. They just have so much more to do because responsibilities sit heavily on their young shoulders. They have to work harder to cement their positions at work and they have to help their family. And, being human, they are in competition with their peers, because while you can try to reconcile with your financial background, it is still not easy seeing people in the same or lesser positions progressing faster than you on a financial level.

Your life can easily start feeling like a series of compromises – your car, house, clothes are not of the standard you desire because you have other financial responsibilities. You work in a high-paying job but you can't buy what you want. You can't enjoy life with abandon and unwind from your stressful job like other colleagues from better financial backgrounds.

The temptation to accept those credit cards and overdrafts that banks are always dangling in front of your eyes soon seems like a way out. After all, you work hard and are paid well, you can manage your line of credit. You start telling yourself you can cover all your financial responsibilities, keep up with the Joneses *and* pay black tax.

As the pressure mounts on black professionals, desperation grows among their unemployed counterparts. Unemployment statistics don't make for good reading. Unemployment is at close to 10 million people and nearly 7 million of those are young black people. As I write this essay at the municipal library in the daytime, there is a constant stream of qualified young black people at the photocopier. They are here to make copies, scan and email their CVs for job applications. You see them every day the library is open.

Education used to be a sure bet for a prosperous future, but here we are today. It was supposed to be a sure thing that the economy would welcome young graduates with open arms. Young people – once the great hope for their families – are confused, they don't know what to do. They feel cheated because they are still jobless after vast sums were paid by struggling parents for them to get an education.

The worst thing is that they feel like liabilities when they have to ask their parents for more money to go out and look for jobs. Keep in mind that for every parent who encourages and supports this unending quest, there are others who don't understand why you can't get a job. If the neighbour's child who didn't even go to university has a job, the problem must be with you. Imagine what that does to the soul of a young person.

Most of the time, parents have begged and borrowed so that their children can to go to university, and some parents also remind their unemployed graduate children of this fact every chance they get. Then these youngsters get desperate and end up applying for any job, even if they have a specialised degree. Anything for an income.

At this point, they often fall into the sadistic trap of casual employment. Money is needed to live so people take whatever comes their way. Dire circumstances force graduates to sign three- or six-month contracts. Families are sustained for a short period but then the contract is not renewed. It is terrible to witness hope dashed in the blink of an eye.

Imagine not having an income for the foreseeable future. It is a terrible way to live.

But people smile and carry on. They do their best under these conditions. These heroes and heroines deserve a round of applause but also better opportunities.

They wake up every day and do their best. They take the little money they earn and make it go a long way. They take the little money they earn and register for other courses. They improve themselves by adding on their qualifications. The sleight of hand with money they witnessed performed by their parents proves to be a hereditary skill. They live off the hope that one day opportunity will knock, looking for a candidate as prepared as they are.

Some people steer clear of black tax. They leave the nest as soon as they make it, never to look back. They progress, buy the finest of material things and post memes with sayings like, 'Your glass must be full first before you can pour for others.'

You look at how much they have progressed and wonder if you would have been able to live with yourself if you had done the same. You recall the heartfelt smile and thank you from a parent or sibling after you had helped them out. You remember that the purpose of helping your parent, sibling or relative is, in fact, an attempt at improving a life. Black people need this financial help we call black tax because chances of spectacular success still come at a premium.

The thing about black tax is that it is an unspoken agreement. There is no promise that the favour you do for others will be returned. You do it without expecting anything in return. You do it no matter how much you want to complain. You do it because it is your duty. Of course, it is bad to see people waste your hard-earned money, but those are exceptions to the rule. Your hard-earned money will, more often than not, really make a difference to others.

A moneyed friend I went to school with puts this issue of black tax into perfect perspective. He graduated with an engineering degree, but jobs were scarce. He decided to start his own company. His parents were sceptical when he decided to take the entrepreneurial route. They wanted him to look for stable employment, but he stuck to his guns. Today, he provides for his family and is putting his siblings through school.

When I asked him how he felt about the heavy financial burden his responsibilities place on him, he said, 'If I don't help out my family, who will?'

Our family backgrounds and family dynamics are never uniform. Neither is the mental outlook of the individual. But there is nothing like a helping hand when you are down and desperate and have nowhere else to turn for help. Some people may think paying black tax is pouring money down the drain, but it is a favour paid forward. The only prerequisite is not that you pay back the one who helped you, but that you assist the next one who needs your help.

'Ingane enhle isebenzela ekhaya.' Keep working for your household, black child.

SIFISO MZOBE is a writer, content editor and translator. His debut novel, *Young Blood*, won numerous awards, including the 2011 Sunday Times Fiction Prize and the 2012 Wole Soyinka Prize for Literature in Africa. He works closely with the Fundza Literacy Trust and has published several short stories on their mobisite, fundza.mobi. Sifiso also mentors young writers. He is currently working on his second novel.

PART 5

Step into my shoes

Tshifhiwa Given Mukwevho

After what seemed like an eternity, the prison doors flew open for me on 11 November 2010 and I stepped out, free at last. Immediately after my arrest, I realised that I had wronged society by breaking into and stealing from numerous business premises in Makhado and that I had to take full responsibility for this and work towards turning my life around.

After 11 years in prison, I felt that I had paid my dues. I came out with some education because I had studied while I was inside, all in preparation for my future, should I live to see the day of my release.

Back in my hometown, Madombidzha village in northern Limpopo, circumstances were such that I found myself waking up each morning and walking to the Muromani crossroads to hitch a lift to town, where I would wander along the streets in the hopes of getting a job of some sort, either from townspeople or with local businesspeople.

I ended up getting work at someone's house as an all-rounder handyman: I cleaned the yard, took care of the garden and washed the nine dogs. Come month-end, however, the madam of the house said she had no money to pay me and suggested that I accept a bicycle which was lying around the yard as payment. I immediately stopped working for this indifferent madam.

Rather than continue being subjected to disrespect and ridicule I started selling snacks on the streets of Makhado town, at the taxi ranks and salons. My stint as a hawker or vendor – pardon the pun, for I remain Venḓa – lasted for about eighteen months.

During this time something wonderful happened: my first book, a collection of short stories entitled *A Traumatic Revenge*, was published. This completely changed how people viewed me, both in town and in the village. Some thought I had instantly become rich, while others said I was on the path to fortune.

The former group found it rather strange that a supposedly rich man would continue to sell snacks at the taxi rank. The latter group suggested that I should stop selling snacks and focus on writing for schools on a full-time basis. They had this idea that when a writer publishes a book it is randomly and instantly prescribed for learners. They also believed I would soon build myself a double-storey mansion like the majority of Tshivenḓa authors who had come before me.

These misconceptions placed me in a difficult position. When I was busy moving up and down the taxi rank selling snacks, an employed brother would come at lunchtime and ask me to buy a loaf of bread, polony and a soft drink for us to share. If I told him I was penniless, he would point at my pockets, bulging with coins and say, 'But here, you've got money.' He would go as far as to suggest that I had even more money from my book sales in the bank and that it was a wrong that I wanted to spend that money alone.

Towards the end of 2011 I started writing features and art reviews for a youth-orientated supplement of a community newspaper. While I was paid for it, I didn't make enough to stop selling snacks. The following year, I started writing for the main newspaper, where I learnt many valuable writing skills.

In 2012, I travelled to Kinross in Mpumalanga to visit Ethokomala School, a reformatory facility for delinquents, where I had also spent some time as a young inmate. It was part of the research for my second book and I wanted to revive my memories of the experiences I had had there. My first novel, *The Violent Gestures of Life*, was published the following year. At that point I stopped selling snacks and focused on selling my books and freelancing for a variety of print and online publications.

It was a big challenge, and frustrating at times, to be a freelance journalist without private transport, and so, a few years later, I bought my first car. I had worked very hard and felt I deserved a skorokoro to make life easier and more enjoyable.

As I drove to town every morning, many men would call my name when I got to the Muromani crossroads, asking me to give them a lift. Whenever I pulled over, three men would fight to get to the passenger seat, while at least seven or more would try to find a spot on the back seat. Eventually, six men would sit on a seat meant for three persons.

All of them were from the same village as me; they are homeboys and homemen. They were all my brothers. To reason with them about the possibility that there could be a roadblock ahead where I ran the risk of being slapped with a

R3 000 fine was futile. All they needed was to get to town so they could hustle for piece jobs. In the evening, after an unsuccessful or successful day of looking for a job, they would walk to Mavhiḓani Cemetery at the entrance to Makhado, a spot from where hundreds of men and women hitched a lift to the villages.

On one occasion my car was full and three more brothers still wanted to force their way in. I explained tactfully that the car was full and there was no more space. Dejected, they stepped back. Then I heard one of them say, 'U vho ri ṱongela ngauri u na goloi!' (He no longer cares about us now that he owns a car!)

One of the men who was outside the car reprimanded him, but the third seconded the first man's comment. I felt quite insulted and disappointed – his words left a sour taste in my mouth.

I decided to drive along Muromani without stopping. I couldn't endure being victimised by my own brothers, so I'd rather not give any of them a lift.

Soon after that day, the car's engine oil started to leak into the radiator. A local mechanic suggested we open the engine and replace a top gasket, but he accidentally interfered with some of the sensitive parts of the engine and that meant the end of the road for my car. I didn't want to waste more money on it, so I had to sell it at the cheapest price.

Without a car, I had to start using public transport again. But once you have tasted the freedom of movement from having your own car, you cannot compromise. Luckily, I managed to save enough to buy another car.

Now, when I passed the Muromani crossroads in the morn-

drink some days ago and that the bottle was still in the car. I rushed into the tavern, bottle in hand, to return it for cash. As I stepped into the tavern, the homeboy who had just asked for a lift took a bottle of zwimeṱemeṱe, or whisky, and a packet of ten Peter Stuyvesant from the teller, along with change of just over R100. As I approached, he was twisting open the cap. I simply proceeded to the counter, handed in the empty bottle and walked out.

Deep in my heart of hearts, I felt cheated. There was no option but to turn around and tactfully whisper into his ear that I did not understand how he could afford to buy a bottle of zwimeṱemeṱe after he had told me he had no money.

His answer was sharp, 'Brother, I need to keep my body warm. I survive on piece jobs. You are a journalist. You've got a real job. You earn a lot of money. You even have a car – something that some of us cannot afford.'

'If you could just step into my shoes,' I wanted to shout at him.

But then again, I thought, he didn't force himself into my car. I still felt a strong urge to give him a piece of my mind, but I turned around and left, my heart torn to pieces. *What does he take me for?*

As I continued, asking myself many questions, my mind drifted to another morning when I had given another brother a lift. I had stopped at the mid-town filling station to fill up, since I was driving to Polokwane and had no intention of stopping anywhere on the way. This brother happened to see some banknotes in my wallet and asked for R50. It is true that I had some money on me, but it was all budgeted for something else.

When I answered that I didn't have money, he stared at me in disbelief and insisted that he had seen the money. I could tell from the tone of his voice that he was not happy; in fact, he was offended. *Perhaps, I was wrong to offer him a lift in the first place*, I thought then.

During my jail term, I stayed in three different prisons, and there are many correctional officers who feel that they directly contributed towards my rehabilitation. Without a doubt, they played an important role and I know each one of them is proud of my journey to rehabilitation and successful reintegration into society. However, when they see me selling my literary publications on the streets, they always ask for signed, complimentary copies because they played an active part in my journey to freedom. To date, for every 100 copies I have taken from my publishers on consignment, at least 38 have gone to my former warders.

Apart from the responsibility I feel towards my community, my immediate family also has many expectations of me. I am the first person to have obtained a university degree in our family, and that, together with the few publications under my name, affords me much respect in our clan. Therefore, whenever there are misunderstandings or fights within the family or clan, I am called in as the mediator. I am supposed to be the wise man, the solver of all problems.

It doesn't end there, though; whenever there are accidents or incidents which require money in order to get addressed, they say, 'Call him. Tell him to come here! There's a funeral again!'

There are many times when I feel like I live in a small, claustrophobic cubicle with no fresh air to breathe. Does a messiah choose to become a messiah? What if too much is expected of me? Why do I sometimes feel so heartbroken, like that man who was put up on a cross?

If only people could step into my shoes, once in a while.

After I completed my Grade 12, I wanted to further my studies. At that time the prolific author of a biblical study series, Michel Barrette, paid me a visit at the Kutama Sinthumule Correctional Centre. He wanted to find out whether I was interested in furthering my studies and I told him I was keen to explore literature.

He offered to pay for my tuition from undergraduate level through to a doctoral degree. I couldn't believe it. This was too much, from a complete stranger. I asked him how I was going to pay him back. He expected nothing, he said, except 'that you may do unto others what I am about to do for you, son'.

Still, there are days when I cannot help wondering where the line is between helping and being taken advantage of.

I cannot but feel guilty when I cannot give something that is being asked of me. Every time I feel too much is being asked, or even *demanded* of me, I remember the help that I got from so many individuals – both inside and outside prison. Then I tell myself that, *maybe*, this is the way that I am supposed to contribute my bit.

TSHIFHIWA GIVEN MUKWEVHO is a novelist, short story writer and journalist. He has written a collection of short stories entitled *A Traumatic Revenge* and a novel, *The Violent Gestures of Life*. He has also published a collection of poems, *It Was Getting Late*. Tshifhiwa is the recipient of a Maskew Miller Longman Literature Award for his children's book, *Mveledzo na Zwigevhenga*. He heads Vhakololo Press, a publishing initiative, in Makhado and lives in Madombidzha village.

As we tithe

Sibongile Fisher

> For the purpose of this essay, let us assume
> that legacy is a gift by will or a curse by inheritance,
> received from an ancestor or the systems of the past.

As your body and your back break, it becomes an inherited curse to break bread. You inherited twice the responsibilities at half the salary but that doesn't matter – if you are lucky enough to be able to pursue a dream then you become the alpha provider.

Black tax is no new phenomenon; it is as real as blood is to bone and has existed since long before the term was coined. The rise of the term, black tax, is tied to the rise of the black middle class. This group is usually made up of those who tried to escape the legacies of apartheid by forging their lives around the slogan 'a better life for all', unaware that 'for all' would mean standing in for what is supposed to be the responsibility of the government.

It is the tithe we pay for having melanin in our skin.

Over the years, black tax has grown exponentially with the rise in the number of black professionals. It wears many faces, most of which we keep mum about. For example, I am taxed for being a woman. In the workplace, I earn less than my male counterparts; I have to work twice as hard to get half of what they get. Now as a *black* woman, I have to work three times as hard to get two-thirds of what they get. I am taxed for being a woman and for being black.

I am both a product and a victim of black tax. As a product, I was raised on black tax. My great aunt – who looked after our whole family – was running the race with the hope that one of us would grow up and help her to retire.

We inherit the gender economics as determined by the forebears of patriarchy and also inherit the racial economics designed by the fathers of capitalism. So, our black tax begins even before we earn our first pay cheques. It begins in our homes, along with the many other things we don't talk about. The unhealthy silences harboured over dinner, on Sundays after church, over Christmas braais and at funerals.

The proverb 'Uk'zala uk'wezelula' and the burden it loads on black children at birth floats as thick as black smoke in our living rooms and we refuse to talk about it. We are silent about how we are seen as investments to be cashed in on later, how we have normalised financial abuse and how, growing up, the one with a promising future becomes the family's contingency plan.

You are trained to grow up with dreams as big as your responsibilities. By the time you join the job market and plan to negotiate your salary – with your parents' arms stretched out, reaching for your first pay cheque – your new employer has already decided how much you should be paid in comparison to your white counterparts, even though you are likely to work twice, or even three times, as hard and with twice the amount of responsibilities.

These are the racial economics you won't be aware of until, on a night out with colleagues, a drunken, slurpy speech slaps your good ear when you overhear them speak about how much they earn. It's not because of their position or their capabilities; because surely your black friend, who is also their senior, still earns less than them. It is because of the unspoken historical scar that continues to stain your country's new image.

In the context of '*South Africa/ We love you/ Oh, our beautiful land/ Let's show the whole world/ we can bring peace in our land*' black tax is a direct legacy of apartheid. It is the systemic offspring which keeps us enchained to our heinous past.

During apartheid, townships thrived on a communal system of survival. This system became our culture and even when the 'rainbow' appeared and we entered the land of 'equal opportunities', we couldn't shake it off. It is in our culture not to watch another suffer, whether that suffering is self-inflicted or caused by the systemic factors that perpetuate poverty.

We are more inclined to help others, because we know that breaking out of poverty is difficult and only the strong-willed get an opportunity to place one foot, or both feet if lucky, on the 'other side' of the beloved country. It feels good because everyone you love won't have to struggle. Not on your watch.

But it's only good when your 'black tax' can afford you privilege. It's not so good when you have to spare half-tigers and pondos to remain part of the family. It's also not so good when you lend your relatives money knowing it will never make its way back to you and when your debit orders start to extend from institutions to people. When you watch how your cousin, who is older than you, squanders her life while you break your body to make a daily living, you tithe – not willingly, but out of a sense of duty.

It is a tax that is both an act of virtue and a vice. Providing for your loved ones is innate but when is it enough? How much is enough? And where does being a provider end and being an enabler begin?

> As a product and victim of black tax: I tithe, I break body, I break bread, I break my back, and I break the bank. I stew in thoughts of the kind of legacy I will leave behind; for my children, for my family and our name, and also, for my race.

You will swallow your words when you speak of it but you do wish to articulate black tax in a way that doesn't make you cry or further batter your already damaged heart because for a child whose parents were miracle workers, a child who had the audacity to dream and to share those dreams at family gatherings and was untouched by the poverty around her, black tax is betrayal.

In your family home, where your childhood was cherished, you chose the liberal arts: stunned, at first, your father will help you search for places to study towards your chosen dreams but then legacy crawls in under his skin and he says, 'Your good grades will not go to waste that way!'

But they do, anyway. You are in your mid-twenties with little to no financial literacy, you need your job or your only option is that you need your job, since your student loan won't pay itself and your mother is banking on your first job as a graduate (after that nonsensical internship where you were expected to survive on transport stipends). Your parents did their best to protect you, to push you forward, to offer you a better life than they had – and they did!

But they couldn't keep you from inheriting the legacy of poverty, the legacy of apartheid and the tithe that ties us to our past – black tax. So, never mind your experience and your capabilities . . . It starts with your name:

'Do you mind if I call you Sibs?'

'Do you think you will vibe with the boys?'

'Do you have a boyfriend, husband or partner?'

'Any kids?'

'Oh, how many?'

And because you are black and a woman, 'Is your boyfriend the father?'

This is another form of black tax we don't speak about, the one that happens in your job interview. You negotiate your blackness and with it you negotiate the tax that is imposed on you by your employer – how much he is willing to offer you, not because of your capabilities, no, but because you are black.

How black are you? Can you afford the privileges of the 'well-spoken' blacks? You don't price yourself too high, lest you don't get hired, because Lord knows beyond the offering baskets, you need the job or the only option is that you need the job.

> We break our backs.
> We break the bank.
> We break our bodies.
> We break bread.

Others rejoice in black tax. They are fulfilled by providing for their loved ones. They find purpose in the reciprocity and for them black tax is a love language. A continual token of appreciation exercised to show their parents and extended families how much they love them. They are devoted to tithing. Their success is rooted in their tithing.

We don't speak of this side of the coin, a side that doesn't recognise black tax, a side that refuses to acknowledge the term, a side that is insulted by its existence. This side believes that black tax is a way of life, a way for black people to survive the raw end of the deal, to survive the cards stacked against us at birth. For them, it is a legacy that has been passed on from one generation to another and 'that's just how our family does things'.

While black tax is a burden to some and a blessing to others, it is a privilege to all. In a sense, it is a 'nice problem' to have. It is better than being on the other end, better than being the one asking. It is a good feeling having the ability to realise your goals and as a consequence, get a space at the table with grownups and other providers.

But this good feeling is fleeting and before you know it, you start paying this tax out of guilt and not out of will. This, at times, can leave you feeling suicidal because after fighting so hard to break out of poverty, breaking your back, body, bank and bread will break you.

I do believe that as we tithe, we also sow the seeds and we can choose to perpetuate the cycle or create new legacies. The more we document and talk about black tax, the more we uncover why it exists and how we can curb it.

SIBONGILE FISHER holds a Higher Certificate in the Performing Arts from the Market Theatre Laboratory and a BCom Degree in Marketing Management. Her short story 'A Door Ajar' won the 2016 Short Story Day Africa Prize and was also shortlisted for the 2017 Brittle Paper Literary Prize and the 2018 Nommo Awards. Sibongile won the 2018 Brittle Paper Literary Award for creative non-fiction for her essay 'The Miseducation of Gratitude'. Her writing has been published in, among others, *Enkare Review, Prufrock* magazine and an anthology, *It Takes Two!* She also chairs The Raising Zion Foundation.

Taking the sting out of black tax

Clinton Chauke

For many black professionals, the financial contributions they have to make to support their extended families eventually turn into a guilt trip. Even though many of them would be happy to 'pay back' those who were instrumental in their upbringing, black tax easily becomes a burden. Why is this? Why can't you do the right thing while getting ahead in life at the same time?

I believe the reason black tax often becomes too heavy a load lies in our education system and the way in which higher education is funded, the salary gap in the workplace between different race groups and the practices of black churches.

The education system of South Africa is very poor. We have too few institutions offering applied and technical qualifications, which means we have fewer competent people who can invent and innovate and advance us technologically. In the end, this also impacts how we advance socially and culturally.

Currently, our education system produces employees instead of employers. The kind of education we receive doesn't encourage us to think big. Rarely, if ever, will you hear someone say, 'I want to start my own company.' Instead, all you hear is, 'I want to work for this big company.' As long as we produce employees, we will never be able to tackle the financial issues at home, because when you are working, you just receive a small portion of whatever business is being dealt with.

If we cannot find ways to improve the education system of South Africa, then there is a price to be paid and it's called black tax.

Furthermore, the way in which higher education is currently funded presents a national crisis. Instead of offering free tertiary education, we rely too much on the National Student Financial Aid Scheme (NSFAS). Not only is the size of this fund too small for the nation's needs, but it is also designed in a way that excludes thousands of students whose parents might earn a salary but are still suffering financially.

Students whose parents have regular jobs – for instance, policemen, nurses and teachers – often do not qualify for NSFAS since the argument is that they can apply for a bank loan. Either way, this means we produce graduates with a lot of debt when they finish their studies. We must not celebrate NSFAS as if it's a generous scheme, we must always remember that it is a loan.

So, on top of their tuition debt, young black professionals who are just starting out in life also have to add a car and often a home loan and life insurance, *and* then they have to take care of their families who are desperately looking to them for financial assistance. The family believes that because the young black professional is earning a steady income, they must have extra money. This is often very far from the truth.

NSFAS itself is a form of black tax because you hardly find any white students on NSFAS. I assume most of them either are able to pay for their studies or have parents who can apply for bank loans.

It is not a coincidence that we have never heard of 'white tax'. This is because the majority of whites receive a good education, many of them are able to pay for the tuition and, once they graduate, they don't rush to leave their homes. Young white graduates don't mind staying with mom and dad in the suburbs until they are financially ready to head out on their own. But black graduates can't stay in the township once they find a job. You have to move out and rent an apartment in town because that's an important measure of success – we have been socialised that way since we were young.

Another reason why there isn't something like white tax is because whites are usually given senior positions in the workplace. This makes them earn higher salaries even when they have lower qualifications. Even today, all the privileges that the apartheid regime bestowed on whites are perpetuated in the workplace.

Because of this the whites are always ahead. In addition, because they come from well-established families, there is no obligation on them to reimburse their parents. They therefore start out with little or no debt and there isn't the extra strain on them to support their parents when they start working.

There is another form of black tax that is often overlooked because it is disguised in the form of an offering at church. In my experience, some pastors manipulate churchgoers into giving a certain amount by claiming that it is the only way to receive redemption. Because they do not know any better or might not be well educated, many people fall for this.

There's an even greater expectation of working churchgoers to contribute money in the form of tithes, offerings and pledges (as separate payments). I have heard pastors who are very critical of youngsters who decide to change churches after they graduate because they groomed them about contributing from a young age, when they were still attending Sunday school. But what really bugs me is that even the unemployed are expected to pledge because they are told this is the only way God will open doors for them.

This year, I went to church for the first time in two years. What a frustrating experience!

Even though I believe in most instances the offerings are used to enrich the pastors, I still found myself standing up to offer. They are so clever in the way in which they present the sermon that even I felt compelled to 'give to the Lord'. That day, the pastor called a lady to the podium; she was wearing glasses and looked like a teacher. She read a few lines from the Bible and then used them in a most creative way to prove that if we didn't offer, we would be robbing God and, of course, if we rob God, he will bring destruction into our lives. She was very intense and passionate when she spoke and it was all quite emotional.

I couldn't help it; I took the last twenty rands I had in my pocket and gave it to her. She had struck such fear into the congregation that many others were doing the same. The choir sang a vibrant song to comfort the flabbergasted souls who were marching to the front to make an offering.

These churches, of course, argue that this is good practice since the money is used to build structures where services could be held or to support the church in other ways. However, it doesn't seem as if the money is used to empower the community.

In this way, religion is used to hold black people back and it becomes another form of black tax.

The biggest responsibility stemming from black tax is usually felt by the first-born child. My eldest sister, Tsakani, is the one who really had to take care of the whole family. She even sacrificed her dream of becoming an engineer because she wanted to provide for the family as soon as possible and a nursing course offered her that, very quickly.

As the last born of my parents' three children, I carry a minimal black tax burden, even though I don't want to pretend that I don't feel the pressure, I did, especially when I had just started working. For instance, when it's somebody's birthday, we are obliged to buy them gifts. If you are a man, you have to do so while you are also busy saving money to pay ilobolo; so much is against you.

Black tax can make you go out every weekend with your friends with the hope of forgetting about your responsibilities or it can make you not go anywhere with the hope of providing for your family. Either way, it is a burden. It is a burden because everyone is looking at you – at times you are even too scared to visit home. It's also painful when you struggle to contribute, because then you just become one of those people who no longer support their parents.

Make no mistake about it, black tax must be paid. Boy, do our parents deserve a breather! In the instance of my mother, you have a lady who has worked really hard to pay tuition fees for her son. So I think she was justified in expecting some money from me after I graduated and secured a job.

What is unjustified is the system's inability to produce the kind of graduate that will be in a position to proudly pay black tax without it being a burden. The underfunding of the education system must come to an end. We need a funding model that will assist the needy who are bright and talented.

The matter of paying blacks very little money must also be addressed and black churches must start to look at the radical ministry of Jesus and stay true to it, without depriving people of their hard-earned money.

Until we resolve these issues, the majority of black people will always be underprivileged and oppressed and black tax will be seen as a curse instead of an opportunity to thank those who helped you get to the top, or at least to a place where you can have access to nice things.

CLINTON CHAUKE is the author of *Born in Chains*, which was longlisted for the Alan Paton Award in 2019, a cheerful, angry 'born free', a hopeless romantic, a proud Mutsonga, an introvert with extroverted tendencies and a guy who aims to change Africa's narration to the world. He reads too much and laughs a lot, especially at things that are not funny, and so forth and so on and things like that.

I must soldier on

Thabiso Mofokeng

Do you know the feeling of being pulled by the balls? Yes, those two balls. When the harder they are being pulled, the louder you scream?

When my sick mother, who was already sick before my father passed away, was taken to the local hospital at Phuthaditjhaba, things immediately started to shift for me. It was expected that I would do everything to ensure that the funeral arrangements went smoothly. I had to be strong for everyone.

At the time, my younger brother was still in primary school in Naledi village. My twin brother, who is a few minutes older than me and was notorious for bathing with Castle Lager, was nowhere to be found.

I won't forget my mother's words in the white male doctor's rooms. 'Doctor, I must be present at my husband's funeral. Please,' she said as she wiped tears from her sunken eyes. 'Who is going to take care of my children?'

The doctor just shook his head and said, 'I'm saving you for your children. It's my final call. I'm transferring you to the hospital. Or do you want to die?'

Stubborn as she is, she had no choice but to abide by the

doctor's decision. In no time, the ambulance was there and took her to hospital. I was thankful because I could see how sitting on the mattress during the mourning period made her condition worse. It didn't help that many of the mourners who came to offer their condolences were telling her they thought it was she who had passed away as she had been looking sicker than her husband.

At home, they were waiting for me.

'Bafana, I don't have taxi fare to my home,' my drunken uncle said, as he let go of the pole at the gate and followed me inside the house. Behind me, I heard him say, 'Your father is no more, it is you who are going to bury me one day.'

Even before the funeral commenced, the village was already packed and many cars had to park very far away from our home. At least the yellowish mud road was clean, thanks to the municipality that had sent a big, yellow TLB (tractor-loader-backhoe) two days before the funeral. It drilled the whole road and filled in the holes with the soil it took from the nearby donga.

I remember it vividly because before I went with the elders to the mortuary, to wash and dress my deceased father, I had to take down the big, wall-mounted clock that almost fell. My maternal grandmother also instructed me to take some of the glasses out of the cupboard, but as I did so, my paternal grandmother started shouting, telling me I was not a girl and shouldn't be doing girl's chores. I didn't know what to do, but fortunately, I was almost done – I stepped out without saying anything. The conflict between my two grandmothers had a long history.

I went into the room with the mattress and picked up a

big, brown envelope. My paternal grandmother had followed me into the room and placed her hands on my head, so I had to bend down a little.

'How much did the funeral policy of my son pay?' she whispered.

'Nkgono, someone is calling me. I will tell you later,' I said and ran out.

After washing my father's lifeless body at the mortuary, we had to go to the parlour to choose the coffin. My uncle nodded as he pointed to one of the more reasonably priced coffins. Even though it was winter, my aunt wiped sweat off her forehead. She shook her head, looked at all of us and wiped her forehead again.

My uncle didn't waste time, 'Rrakgadi, what is it? Is something wrong?'

We all looked at her. The manager of the funeral parlour went outside to give us some privacy.

'My brother worked hard for himself. There's no way we are going to choose this cheap thing. Either we go for the casket or the dome!'

My father's uncle looked at all of us and said, 'I think you are right.'

My uncle didn't agree with them, 'Yes, I know he worked for himself but there must be something left for his family. What are they going to survive on when we do this?'

Then they all looked at me.

'How about we at least take a casket?' I said. They nodded.

'As you can see, it is R18 000, including our reliable fleet, flowers, colourful programmes and the tent,' the smiling manager said. 'What about the funeral time? We have an eight to ten in the morning and a one to three in the afternoon.' Before anyone could say anything, I chose eight to ten – the earlier the better.

The following day, the tent was erected very early in the morning. Men got ready for their work: sharpening their knives to slaughter a cow in the afternoon. They also went to the cemetery to dig a grave. Women peeled vegetables. The corpse arrived. They wailed and wailed.

My twin brother finally faced the reality that our father was no more. You could see that he was feeling cold, but he didn't bother to wear something warmer. He also didn't bother to eat. I still had no idea where he had been during the busiest days of that week. My brother was not really fond of me. Although we started school at the same age, I finished before him and he also thought I was my mom's favourite. He once told me so when he was drunk.

The vigil took place. The long night of winter was very short. Then the funeral proceedings took place. Everything happened so quickly.

After the funeral several people came to us, the children of the deceased, and said that if we needed anything, they were just a phone call away. A few hid themselves from us, we didn't even see them depart. Others, while specifically looking at me, told us that we were now the men of the family and that they depended on us. Many asked me for taxi fare, even those who came from far, like Bloemfontein and Vereeniging.

The next morning at dawn I woke up, my body feeling heavy. I wasn't even fully awake yet when I remembered the small, brown bag with the money that was left over. I quickly got up and looked around. I was relieved to find it on the floor, but when I picked it up, it was light as a feather. The money was gone.

I suspected my brother, who had come home drunk the evening before. When I confronted him, he told me I was busy making myself a boss in the family.

After two weeks my mother was discharged from hospital. They had finally diagnosed her with TB. She was put on a six-month treatment programme at the clinic, where a nurse would give her medicine daily. We tried to get her a sick pension, but the state doctor said she didn't qualify, even though she was not able to do anything. People in our village thought my mother was HIV positive; they gossiped about her for a long time.

Although she was happy to see us and to be home, I noticed that she regretted it because there was no food. Her mother came to take care of her. She, my mother, was very grateful when she found out that she was the main beneficiary of my father's assets.

My paternal family, however, was furious. They told me several times that if my mother thought she could spend their son's money and use the house while they were still alive, she should think again. As we were living in the same yard with my paternal family, my paternal aunt and paternal grandmother decided to come and move in with us. There were now seven of us in the house.

I was already falling behind with my LLB degree modules but I totally lost focus when I received a letter stating the outstanding balance. There was no money to settle it, so I decided to abandon my studies. My priority was to pay for electricity and food so that my mom could take her medicine on a full stomach.

I had to soldier on. So I went from village to village looking for gardening jobs. I planted maize. I sowed potatoes. I cleaned yards and took care of chickens and ducks. Sometimes, I was paid with a plate of food. I also started to plant spinach at home to sell.

My paternal grandmother would sometimes buy us chicken feet and heads the day she received her pension. The rest of the money would go to support her other children's families. My maternal grandmother would try to buy some vegetables. She used the remaining money to pay for medical treatment and to buy food for the family of her son, who had passed away several years ago.

My mother was slowly responding positively to her treatment. She was beginning to walk with the help of a stick.

During this time, I grew very close to my maternal grandmother. We joked together and she supported me in my dream of becoming a writer. I shared some of my handwritten short stories with her. She would often tell us how tired she was and she started singing a song about returning to her home. We would tease her and say we won her, so she was not going anywhere. She said she had completed her task.

My grandmother started to feel dizzy and she would sleep regularly during the day. She even lost interest in her favourite soapie, *Muvhango*. One afternoon, I came home from town after I had spent the whole day looking for a cheap internet café where I could type my first manuscript. The repeat episode of *Muvhango* was on and I told my maternal grandmother, but she shook her head slowly and stayed in bed.

After *Muvhango*, my mother and I watched another show before my mother got up to check on my grandmother. She returned with tears streaming down her face. All she said was, 'What did I do to deserve this?'

My grandmother was buried at her home. My mother spent some weeks there and finally came back to our home. Of course, we would no longer receive my grandmother's pension payout but I made sure that there was something for my brothers to eat while my mother was trying to heal. But I know her, I could see she was struggling.

My paternal grandmother and aunt decided to leave us. We really began to feel the gap left by my father. We pretended to be okay but, in fact, it was unbearable.

One afternoon, while I was washing my late father's old car, I played the song 'Remember Me', by Lucky Dube. Suddenly, my aunt stopped the music. I became angry, dropped the washing cloth on the mud floor and went to report her to my mother, only to find my mother in tears. The song had hit her hard because it was a song she and my father used to listen to and sing together.

As time went by, one of our neighbours arranged a 12-month learnership for me at the municipality and I started interning at the hospital. For some reason, I didn't get my first salary but I was not allowed to dig deeper into the matter. When I finally got my salary the following month it was R1 999 – not nearly enough for all of us.

For additional income, I started selling brown beans and my mother baked cakes in order to help me. At least, mom had decent meals for her medication. Her treatment was almost over. My younger brother had pocket money to take to school. My twin went job hunting after he passed Grade 12.

I tried to pay for my study modules again, doing one module every six months.

After a year, my learnership came to an end. So I volunteered at the hospital in the hope of getting hired. On the 15th of each month, colleagues would knock off early, leaving me in charge of the big offices. Even with my little experience, I applied several times at government institutions, but without any success.

I had to soldier on, and so I decided to focus on my writing career. I used the little money I had saved to type my first short story. I hiked, getting lifts in trucks and sleeping at a prison, to attend my first writing workshop in Bloemfontein, about 400 kilometres from home. I also went all out to meet the veteran Sesotho writer Dr KPD Maphalla, who hired me as his casual secretary. He also helped me to submit a short story to Maskew Miller Longman.

My short story was published – it was one of the best things that had happened to me in years. I contacted publishers and I enquired about working in the industry as it was my dream to work at a publishing house. Sadly, there weren't any opportunities, but I continued to write and taught myself to edit Sesotho works. I also registered a publishing and book distribution company.

But then I had a major setback when TB knocked me down. I was put on an eight-month treatment programme. I am convinced that the stress of me and my family not having enough was one of the reasons I fell ill.

After I had recovered, I did editing jobs for a number of

reputable publishers. The little I earned from this I took home. Sometimes, when things were tough, I was embarrassed to go home. My finances were always going up and down. Not being able to provide for my family hurt me a lot.

There were times when I thought of disappearing and going to live elsewhere. I also thought about killing myself. My family depended on me financially and emotionally, but I was dying inside. What killed me even more is that I couldn't tell them, particularly my mother, that I needed a break.

After my father's pension fund paid out, things were a little better for a while, but that money didn't last long because it was used to pay his debts and to renovate the house. Hard days were upon us again.

At some point I spent a few days at my girlfriend's place but then I decided I didn't want to go back home again. I told myself that God had chosen me to help others who were not my family. I knew this was hurting my family, but I felt I first needed to heal from the many things that had happened to me. I found it hard to visit home and especially to relate with my paternal relatives.

I won't forget the day I had had enough of everything. The day my dark, red blood was the only thing my eyes saw. It felt like my breath was being pressed back into my lungs. But here I am – still trying to understand what saved me that day.

This unforgettable scene happened on the tenth of some month. The due date for the rent was the seventh and I couldn't pay. I'd spent all my money buying a fridge for my mom, because the old fridge didn't do its job anymore. I had to act, right?

I was hoping to get a payment at the end of the month for some editing work I'd done. I would stare at my phone all day, waiting for the bank notification, and jump up when a message came in, only to find it was some or other annoying message. After a few days, I started thinking my bank account was not linked to my cellphone number anymore.

Throughout this time the landlord was looking for me, looking for his money. During the day I would lock the security gate and the door of my room and take out the key so no one could see I was around. The window was also tightly closed. After all, in Phuthaditjhaba's townships, everyone minded their own business.

One day I could hear the landlord's footsteps outside. He banged on the door with his big fist, but I kept quiet and didn't make a move. I won't forget his insults. During the night, when I could hear there was no one outside, I would sneak out to go to the toilet.

The following day, just as the landlord was about to break the window, I got a bank notification. I quickly opened the curtain. For a moment, he seemed surprised to see me but then he started swearing at me. I slowly opened the door.

'If you don't give me my money now, you are out!' he cried.

I told him I was sick but that I would go to the nearby ATM to get his money. When I returned, I found him waiting on my doorstep. He pointed at me and told me this had better be the last time I was late with the rent. That was the day I just wanted to give up, the day I felt I was being pulled by the balls.

My company continued to show some progress and I could pay myself a salary of a thousand rands or so when there were sunny days. Whenever some money came in, I would notify my family and relatives, but instead of celebrating my success with me, all they would do is tell me about their financial needs. At the time, I just needed someone to be happy for me.

I know very well that charity begins at home, but sometimes 'home' can make things really difficult for you. Whenever there is a death in the family, I am expected to help with everything. Often, I go the extra mile and ask for loans just to protect our clan's name. At the end of the month, the notifications of the debit orders of relatives' funeral policies don't stop beeping on my phone. But what can I do? Many of my family members don't even bother to insure themselves and they are proud to say I will bury them.

I ended up not being able to service and insure my car. I ended up not being able to stick to my budget. I also ended up being closer to the strangers who don't know my background than to my family.

One of the most important things I've since learnt is that you need to teach people how to catch fish. And if they are not eager to learn how to catch fish, I can only respond with the saying, 'You are not required to set yourself on fire to keep other people warm'.

Although I made the decision to approach my family commitments in this way some time ago, I have already started to regret it. Consequently, I frequently lend a helping hand wherever I can. If I don't help them, who will?

I keep telling myself, I must simply soldier on.

THABISO MOFOKENG is a lover of all forms of art. His sense of creativity fuelled his passion for writing and his love of languages fuelled his passion for publishing and language services.

I must soldier on

He was born and bred in Naledi village, in the eastern Free State, where he used to look after his grandfather's cattle by the river and on the mountains. It was there that he realised nature brings peace and everlasting hope.

The Black Tax Club

Mohale Mashigo

A sense of achievement was in the air at the annual gathering. Trucks lined up outside the same house and us in our little car. Waiting.

There were some new faces, but I was always relieved to see so many of the old faces smiling and chatting. They knew my name, but I respectfully referred to everyone as Ausi Somebody or Abuti Someone.

Christmas and New Year had passed, which meant I would have to go back to school soon. This was something I always looked forward to after the New Year's celebrations. It was like a second Christmas, there were snacks and drinks for all who gathered there. The festivities made me forget about having to go back to school. The curious neighbours watched on, even though they saw this happen every year.

Once everyone's names had been ticked off the register, the process began in earnest. The first truck was the one filled with edibles: canned food, mielie meal, biscuits, tea etc. Everything was divided up carefully between the stokvel members. Husbands and brothers took the food and started loading it into cars. Some members had organised a van to share, so they waited for their driver to put the boxes into the hired vehicle.

The second truckload contained cleaning equipment, detergent, roll-on, body lotion, toothpaste, toilet paper etc. Again, things were loaded into vehicles until it looked like there was no space in the vehicles for the passengers. My father would always leave a little space for me to sit and I would put small packages on my lap. It made me feel useful.

I preferred to stay in my father's old Ford Cortina; not that I had much of a choice. Ma had already warned me to stay out of the way. From the back seat of my father's car, I could see all the women in the Grocery Stokvel chatting, shouting orders and making sure their goods were ticked off a list – once they had been collected.

The Grocery Stokvel was mainly made up of women and it kept many of their extended family members from going hungry. Every month the stokvel members would put away a small amount of money. With this money they would buy stamps from a supermarket. At the beginning of a new year, with most items going on sale, they would buy non-perishables in bulk, fill up a truck and divide it among themselves. Any money they had left would be dedicated to school supplies, fees and uniforms.

Most of them were people who couldn't afford to save but, somehow, they did. At the time, I didn't understand the magic that these women made from absolutely nothing, but I do now.

My mother was in her early thirties, married and living in her late mother's house in Mapetla, Soweto. Her prospects of furthering her education had died when she selflessly decided to look after her elderly mother. Nothing is new under the sun – not even the sacrifices we make.

> What's in a name? That which we call a rose
> By any other word would smell as sweet.
> – Juliet, in *Romeo & Juliet*, Act II Scene ii

I'm obsessed with names. It is impossible for me to write a story if I haven't given the protagonist a name. This obsession with names almost cost me my first novel; there was no way I could write a story about someone whose name didn't fit.

My best friend's mother had a theory that when you're given a name, it affects who and what you become even if you don't realise it. She took my name, Kgomotso, which means comfort, by way of example. My maternal grandmother had died shortly before I was born so my birth brought my mother great comfort.

I recently found out that there is an actual name for this phenomenon: Nominative Determinism. It's an important sounding term, but not quite as poetic as the words of my best friend's mother.

I keep a book of different names and their meanings – whenever I encounter an interesting name, it goes straight into my book of names. Naming things makes them appear clearer to me. Which brings me to the name of this club most of us belong to.

'Black tax' is something that has become a part of our lexicon. I don't know when the term was birthed or by whom. Perhaps we had been eating and drinking air, instead of solids and liquids, for so long that the pressure on our collective oesophagus became too much and we belched 'black tax'.

When I started writing about black tax, I was reminded of the Grocery Stokvel. In many regards all of us who pay black tax belong to a similar kind of club. It's a club where you don't have to explain your origin story – my mother died when I was 11 – or explain the rules – I *have* to look after my niece. Someone close to you would've introduced you to it.

This club makes us feel less alone – it also makes us want to fight the unjust systems that drove us into this club. Let's just call it the Black Tax Club.

However, unlike the people who were part of Fight Club, in the movie of that name, there's nothing exclusive or secretive about the Black Tax Club.

Both the first and the second rule of Fight Club says, 'You *do not* talk about Fight Club.' This rule does not apply to the Black Tax Club, because black tax is such a popular topic on Sunday Twitter. Unlike Fight Club, black tax and the rules of belonging to the Black Tax Club are something we can and must talk about.

However, there is something about the term black tax that doesn't sit well on my tongue or in my chest. The words follow each other a little too closely and in an accusatory manner. The indictment is also often aimed at the wrong people.

> BEE is here and you're still broke?
> Your parents suffered and you're still living at home?
> How can you earn so much and still be broke come mid-month?
> Why do you spoil your family members by paying their bills?
> You don't have savings?

The term 'non-fulfilment tax', however, sings a different tune. It sings a song about the legacy of hateful people who didn't consider black people human. This particular ditty is in three-part harmony featuring vocals from these hateful people, corrupt politicians (post 1994) and the private sector (one of the many monikers of the superstar, capitalism).

'Non-fulfilment tax' speaks to broken promises made by the people in power – they simply failed to do what they had said they would do. We should be pointing the finger at those who created the situation we find ourselves in and to their successors who opted to continue being a failure.

Like Fight Club there's a certain violence to belonging to the Black Tax Club. This legacy of fighting for your life at work and carrying your family to bed with you is demoralising and weighs heavy on a young person. Today, the jobs have better titles and the graduation photos are there but the rules of black tax say we are one mistake away from ending right back where our parents or grandparents began.

It is also inhumane that people who ought to be retired should be forced to continue working because their adult children and grandchildren can't find employment.

Since I'm borrowing rules from Fight Club let's examine their third rule:

> 'If someone yells "stop", goes limp or taps out, the fight is over'

The Black Tax Club is a generational thing. It is a family member losing a job and relying on his or her elderly parents to take them in, sometimes with their nuclear family. My own parents went into Black Tax Super Saiyan Mode when they discovered that I was unable to work because of severe depression and generalised anxiety disorder. They may not have understood my illness, but they sent money and even summoned me home.

At my grown-up age, I was one mental breakdown away from losing it all.

Black tax also means always being at risk of feeling like a disappointment because you couldn't lift the curse and somehow became part of it. You can yell, tap out or rage, and still the ghost of non-fulfilled government promises will haunt your family. There are plenty of articles that claim to provide 'hacks for black tax' when the truth is there is no hack. The fight continues.

Fight Club rule 4: 'Only two guys to a fight'

Shame is the mother of isolation but remember that you are not alone. The shame burns hot when we think about our counterparts who buy homes, go on overseas trips annually, send their children to better schools – they aren't living and fighting. Living looks good on them. In this fight there are not only two people in the ring, the Black Tax Club is made up of millions of people fighting one opponent who does not fight fair.

Fight Club rule 5: 'One fight at a time'

At times, the Black Tax Club requires of you to multi-task. You often have to fight many fights, all at once. You need to be Ali (Laila), Stone Cold Steve Austin and an MMA fighter while you're working on getting your Brazilian jiu-jitsu red belt.

When the topic of black tax comes up there are always many opposing viewpoints on Sunday Twitter. Some feel it is an extension of ubuntu – 'If you don't look after your people, who will?' – while others argue that reparations are necessary and that whites should 'give back the land'. Then there are also those who mention the abuse endured at the hands of a family who treat you like either a leech or a cash cow.

I was fighting many battles in 2018. The proverbial dam burst when friends suggested I seek help. I was severely depressed and didn't realise it because I was in the 'ring' fighting too many fights. Sometimes the Black Tax Club makes Fight Club seem like a walk in a park.

I stayed up many nights worrying about those I care about, my progress in life, about possibly losing my apartment, about what would happen if I got sick or if my parents got sick, etc. It felt like I had inherited the wounds of people before me and they had begun to fester. There was no differentiating between my worries and those brought on by my membership of the Black Tax Club. And this from the perspective of someone who is employed.

According to Statistics South Africa, 'The burden of unemployment is also concentrated amongst the youth as they account for 63,5% of the total number of unemployed persons. The unemployment rate among the youth is higher irrespective of education level.'[1] It doesn't take a genius to make a connection between the stats, black tax and the mental health of young people in our country. We are fighting many fights at a time and sometimes it seems as though we are not winning.

> Fight Club rule 8: 'If this is your first night at Fight Club, you have to fight'

I've skipped all the way to the last rule of Fight Club because this analogy is making me sad. It's sad because the Black Tax

Club is something you're born into; you don't have a real choice in the matter. You are expected to fight from the minute you are inducted into the club. This almost always means you will have anxiety, about money, for a long time.

Keep fighting; whether you're fighting off the shame, or fighting to work through your financial anxiety, or fighting to get out of the club to cure a generational malady.

And if you've made it out of the Black Tax Club, please fight the urge to judge those who haven't.

> Really, living at home and you're 29?
> She's just waiting to inherit her grandmother's house instead of working for her own.
> What kind of adult doesn't have a car?

This brings me to a related point – this Eurocentric idea that there is a specific time to move out of your family home is strange. A family home is exactly that; a home for a family. Ours is constantly filled with other members of the family. If you can afford to move out, do it. But leaving home at a certain age should not be an indication of how well you're doing. I mean that sincerely.

My mother was of the opinion that I should first move out once I'm married. She only allowed me to leave home because I went to university in another province and then found a job in yet another. Even now she insists that I should move back.

We inherit these homes because they belong to our people. There is no one person who is responsible for the upkeep of the house. There are those who shine the floors and stoep, those who are good with their hands and gently fix an ageing house and others who fill the cupboards with food. Children fill it with life and laughter.

There is no waiting to inherit a house that you live in. It is your home and we need to think of ownership in a different way. Of course, there are greedy relatives who will try to 'hijack' a house to sell or live in it. I would go as far as saying that it is a horrible side-effect of being part of a club that knows the land but owns so little of it.

My first family home was in Mapetla and it was the house my mother and her siblings lived in with their parents. Our family then took it over because my mother was the last family member left in it with her mother. My parents never thought of transferring ownership, it was our family home.

Eventually, an uncle decided to lay claim to it and we moved to what is now our family home in a different part of Soweto. Had greed and sheer thuggery not kicked us out of that house, we would have worked on making it bigger for our growing family.

One of the people I follow on Twitter, Nomantshali Ninise, once tweeted something that stayed with me for a long time. I am paraphrasing, but she said, 'Being poor means you always have to explain your circumstances to people.'

In a strange shaming exercise, certain South African oligarchs also have a lot to say about young black people buying expensive cars. This subject is so tired. Can we just let it walk outside and die like the old dog that it is?

To the oligarchs I want to say, please, *hou op!* Stop making us explain and maybe listen to us instead. Nobody knows this club better than its members. It must be difficult to let someone else have the floor, but try it.

There is no twist at the end of the story of the Black Tax Club. In fact, it ends pretty much the same way as the annual gathering of the Grocery Stokvel. We all drive away feeling quite pleased that we made it through another year.

The air in the car is filled with the strong smell of all the soap packed next to me, Pa is whistling and Ma is already insisting we go through everything carefully when we get home. Some things will be shared with my aunt and our neighbours (in weeks to come). Even though we know we will be okay for a few months, there is still that sense of dread.

While I sigh because the school holidays are nearly over, in the back of their minds, my parents are already starting to worry about whether they will have to scrape money together again during the next year. Away our little family drives with a car full of groceries and hopes that promises will be fulfilled so we can live the South African dream without also living by the rules of a violent club.

Rule number one of the Black Tax Club: We can and will continue to talk about it until it's history.

MOHALE MASHIGO is the author of the widely acclaimed and bestselling novel *The Yearning*, which won the University of Johannesburg 2016 Debut Prize for South African Writing in English. Her latest offering is *Intruders*, a collection of (speculative fiction) short stories that explore how it feels not to belong. Mohale is also a comic book writer and an award-winning singer-songwriter.

Note

1 'Youth unemployment still high in Q1: 2018', see http://www.statssa.gov.za/?p=11129.

PART 6

A monument to the survival of the African family

Monde Nkasawe

The words 'black tax' throw into sharp relief an image where one's relatives stand at the ready, waiting to pounce on your first pay cheque. For many, it is as unwelcome as it is unavoidable – a concept that evokes strong emotion; often, deep resentment.

One can almost hear the biblical Abel desperately asking, 'Am I my brother's keeper?' At best, black tax is a burdensome reality, at worst, it can be a crisis of conscience concerning the validity of one's familial connections.

To put it plainly, black tax is the coercion of gratitude.

But what, exactly, is black tax? How does it manifest itself in practice? Is it wrong? Is it right?

I will attempt to answer these questions, not to establish an all-time definition, but to illustrate what I think it actually represents. In the process I shall make reference to four broad themes, namely: some of the known excesses of black tax, the historical context in which it may be understood, rural and urban migration dynamics in which are embedded the notion of familial support, and social change with its impact on black communities.

Black tax has many permutations and variants and it takes

place in almost equal measure in both rural and urban settings. The gist of it is that a young person starting his or her life after slogging through school and university is permanently expected to show 'gratitude' for all the support received from relatives. We also know that black people feel it the most, although I'm not quite sure, and it's not the purpose of this article, if its burdens are not felt by white people.

While there may not be a single definition of black tax, it touches on some of the following points: the need to insulate against and survive economic hardships, the yearning to belong, payment for support received, the alienating impact of urbanisation, the growing schism between rural and urban lives, the cost and styles of living and the foundational values of ubuntu, as well as formal state taxation and the add-on effect of paying black tax.

Another important issue that also comes into play is transport costs. The legacy of our segregated past means that most black people live a good distance away from their places of work, with some having to wake up very early in the morning and use about five modes of transport before they get to work.

Then, there's the impact of the 'two homes' concept; namely, the home in the city and the ancestral home in the village.

Regardless of its exact definition, an essential characteristic of black tax is an aspect of emotional blackmail, one that says, 'anything else you do will be cursed if you forsake your family'.

To illustrate this point, let us take the case of a young woman who gets her first job in the big city, and has to leave parents, siblings and relatives behind at the rural village home. As soon as she gets her first salary, a big chunk of that money is expected to go to her parents and whoever else remains at home, sometimes regardless of whether or not they actually need it.

Soon after settling in at her job, this young person is followed into the city by her siblings, relatives and their children, and instantly she has to perform the role of parent, with all the responsibility that goes with it. Her small city accommodation is soon overcrowded with people that she is expected to support from the same salary that is also supporting her parents and other relatives in the village. The needs of the stay-in siblings begin to expand, and soon she has to pay for their school fees, buy food and clothes for them and even pay for their incidental expenses.

Social problems, being the reality that they are, often mean that this young person's siblings will start having their own children whilst living with her, with all the drama of baby mamas and absent fathers that come with it. If none of them are working, as tends to happen, they will all fully expect their hapless young benefactress to take care of all their needs.

In time, this young professional person will probably fall in love and have children of her own and even get married. But the idea that she may be needing space for her partner and own children is rendered mute by the fact that everyone who bears her surname regards themselves as family, and her house as their home, with a certain sense of entitlement. In fact, her in-laws, if she gets married, may too become her burden.

But still, this is not all. This young woman is also expected to support the maintenance and upkeep of her parents' rural home, with everything that breaks promptly reported to her – the garden fence has collapsed, the kitchen needs fixing, new dishes, cups and water buckets must be bought because all the others got 'lost' at next door's umgidi, a bull is needed to mate with the cow and piglets must be bought for rearing.

Everything you can think of is added on the lady's expense list, willy-nilly. I have even heard of instances where a family member, a father or a close uncle, will take their car in for major repairs and then ask the young working person to pay the bill.

As if that was not enough, there are also endless and expensive cultural and ritual activities which the family cannot avoid, and because she is the only one who is working, they are by default also at her expense. If there happens to be a funeral, everybody will just fold their arms and expect her to buy the coffin, the cow and sheep that must be slaughtered and the groceries. To pour salt on her wounds, even though they have not made any contribution to the expenses, this will not stop her relatives from pointing out that the coffin must not be embarrassingly cheap, that the slaughtered animals cannot be too lean, that there should be flowers and a band, and that everyone must be served fizzy drinks.

Sometimes the young lady will take burial society insurance for all members of her family, which means she must commit to long-term premium payments. If a family member is sick and needs to be taken to hospital, even when an ambulance is called, the young person will also be contacted. Even when there is no crisis whatsoever, the demand for money is unrelenting, and it becomes clear that what everybody wants from her is more than support. They want their cut.

What I have described above are some of the known excesses of black tax. In cases like this, the overriding idea when a young person finds a job is that they should know that it is their extended family who are 'deploying' them to their job, *'and therefore the job is not yours to do with as you please'*.

Practised like this, black tax is as unfair and merciless as it is predatory. The family preys on its own kind and it's never enough.

Could the young woman not simply refuse, you ask? She can resist and she can complain, but to refuse completely is not an easy option. It is akin to opting out of society, because the 'punishment' for refusing to pay black tax is indirect but swift and decisive. You'll be ostracised by family and relatives who will accusingly say, 'Ucing'ba ubhetele, uzidla ngemali, awunambulelo, lento!'

This kind of condemnation and even downright hatred will ensure that people continue to pay black tax, because you want to remain connected to your roots and you want your children to be accepted.

To appreciate the nature of black families in terms of how they are structured and also the source of their fervent wishes today, one has to understand the historical context of families in South Africa.

From the 17th century, black communities, who at that time were living as pristine, hunter-gatherer societies who eked out a living on the land, suddenly had to deal with intruding settlers, and cope with slavery and full-blown colonisation. In the past 100 years they have had to stand up against apartheid, both defeating it and being changed by such a struggle.

A major consequence of all these changes was the breakup of the African family structure, especially in the period following the discovery of diamonds in Kimberley and gold in the former Transvaal, which also gave rise to the growth of industries in Johannesburg. This increased industrialisation required cheap labour. There were several deliberate, systemic and sustained efforts over time to ensure that cheap, African labour was available.

For example, a great deal of compulsion and coercion happened through taxation, such as the dog tax, the hut tax, etc, all of which were aimed at compelling able-bodied men to leave the countryside and go to the mines and manufacturing industries. Recruitment schemes such as The Employment Bureau of Africa (TEBA) forced millions of young men to leave their homes to go and work on the mines, leaving their wives, children, siblings and parents to survive on subsistence farming.

These coercion methods were intended to ensure that Africans were taken off the land and compelled to work for a living by earning money, failing which their families would starve. Hence was born the notion of imali ndiyithobile (sending money home).

A proper investigation of the issue of black tax, therefore, needs to consider the historical position of the rural African family and the colonial, ideologically driven quest to dismantle it. The agrarian transformation of the countryside and the intensification of industrialisation in urban centres are perhaps the two most impactful social change events in our country, which account for most of the destruction visited on the African family structure.

At the beginning of the colonialist project to settle in South Africa, whites were heavily dependent on black farmers through sharecropping for their economic survival. But, as Timothy Keegan writes in *Rural Transformations in Industrializing South Africa: The Southern Highveld to 1914,*

> sharecropping relationships between white and black farmers were never regarded as legitimate in the dominant perceptions of whites. Sharecropping on the farms was largely practised outside of formal civil sanctions and prescriptions (which also explains the paucity of documentary or statistical evidence on such relationships). Whites were generally very reluctant to admit that they were so 'degenerate' as to rely on 'Kaffir farmers', and dominant populist ideology was fiercely antagonistic to any form of black economic independence. This factor provided much of the impetus behind the drive to suppress black sharecropping by legislation, and the drive by various governments to pour large sums of capital into white farming.[1]

In a contribution published in *South African Capitalism and Black Political Opposition*, ML Morris also writes: 'The development of capitalist production relations elsewhere, mainly in mining in the late 19th century, and the consequent creation of a larger home market began a process of rapid transformation of the social relations of production in the countryside. Production of agricultural commodities for the home market was given a major boost, and many landowners shifted the source of their income away from rent to the sale of their farm produce. Integral to this was a process of eliminating the African peasantry and transforming it into a source of farm labour.'[2]

In fact, according to Mahmood Mamdani, as part of 'native administration', a Native Treasury was established from which the salaries of traditional leaders would henceforth be paid. He notes that early legislation 'had invited chiefs – most likely out of practical considerations – to share with government authorities whatever dues, fines and fees they had collected'.[3]

When Mamdani expands on this argument, he points out that the salary levels of chiefs were determined on the basis of the amount of tax they were able to collect rather than on the number of people under their administration. This led to a situation where chiefs, eager to augment their salaries, resorted to extortion. The tax, which was paid directly into the newly created treasury, became a measure by which to bypass all forms of tribute, further adding pressure on numerous men to abandon their homes and seek formal employment.

The view is also advanced by TRH Davenport when he observes the same pattern of destruction of African traditional systems. He notes that, when Charles Griffith was appointed as High Commissioner in Lesotho in 1871, he immediately set about 'the reduction of chiefly power with determination, notably by the introduction of a hut tax (which the chiefs were required to collect in return for an honorarium) and the suppression of the obligatory labour service (Letsema) which . . . had become burdensome in recent years.'[4]

Blogger Sifiso Mkhonto, writing for News24, states that black tax is a legacy of the apartheid system brought into our democracy intentionally. He also argues that black tax is not a burden, but a responsibility.[5]

Today, we have to deal with a very sad legacy of displacement, with almost all towns in South Africa characterised by the same spatial feature of tiny, matchbox-type homes and shacks (one can add male hostels in most major cities). As explained above, this concentration of people in urban areas was not a natural outcome of economic factors but was deliberately engineered.

For all these historical reasons the phenomenon of black tax becomes a political one. It recalls the words of Steve Biko, who said, 'Black man, you are on your own,' and, in a sense, it encourages black solidarity and black consciousness.

The disruptive intrusion of colonialism on the original African manner of living produced a survivalist reaction – black tax, where family members support each other in their efforts to improve their lot. Notwithstanding its excesses, black tax can be seen as an attempt to counter the historic intention of white colonial settlers to decimate the African family structure. To a very large extent, colonialism actually failed in this regard, thanks, in no small measure, to black tax in all its forms.

In one very important respect, black tax is also a poverty alleviation initiative. One of the reasons it can feel like such a burden, apart from the financial implications, is the knowledge that to stop paying would have the effect of immediately condemning family members to days without food. 'Isandla sihlamba esinye,' so goes an isiXhosa saying – 'one hand washes the other' – which is complemented by another saying, 'Umntu ngumntu ngomnye umntu.'

What is meant by all of this is that there will be those who will carry you on your way to success, but with a corollary obligation – you will have to carry them, too. However, it is an expectation originally founded not on greed but on the desperate experience of history and suffering.

Black tax is also an apt illustration of the poverty value chain in contemporary society. It reflects a tension between the individualising logic of urban existence and the communitarian roots from which most of us have emerged in the country's hinterlands.

In the manner in which 'success' has come to be defined, each family has a mission – to get out of poverty and to 'succeed'. This mission to succeed is pursued with vigour and all earnestness, energy and single-minded purpose. It is a mission reflected in the prayers of the elderly, in the names given to children, such as Vusumzi (reawaken or revive the family home), Mpumelelo (success) and Mandla (strength). This mission to 'succeed' is all-consuming, and families send their children to school not to seek knowledge for its own sake, but to give their children a competitive edge in the world of work. Families have dreams, which manifest as the quest for finer things in life.

Of course, these dreams are not always matched by the equal effort of all. There are slackers who live off the efforts of others. In a number of instances, a family member will sit at home, showing no initiative or inclination of any kind whatsoever, but will expect to be given money and material support, purely on the strength of familial relationship. This has given black tax its bad name, perhaps unfairly so.

I believe that black tax is an alternative form of social security for black people. In a very revolutionary respect, black tax represents a form of pushback and rebellion against attempts to annihilate the nucleus of the African family. Despite the many ways in which it has been abused, it has also succeeded in keeping black familial connections from wholesale colonial destruction.

With scars of different kinds, the African family, culture and languages have survived colonial settler intrusion as well as the machinations of apartheid. Black tax stands as a monument to this.

MONDE NKASAWE is the author of eight books, including several novels and a volume of poetry. His novels include *The Death of Nowongile, The Fullness of Time* and, most recently, *We Need a Country*. After completing a master's degree in history, Monde became a government official working in many different departments. He is currently a Chief Director in the Office of the Eastern Cape Premier.

Notes

1 Keegan, TJ. *Rural Transformations in Industrializing South Africa: The Southern Highveld to 1914*. 1986. Braamfontein: Raven Press.
2 Morris, ML. 'The development of capitalism in South African agriculture: class struggle in the countryside' in *South African Capitalism and Black Political Opposition*. 1982. Cambridge and Massachusetts: Schenkman.
3 Mamdani, M. *Citizen and Subject: Contemporary Africa and the Legacy of Late Colonialism*. 1996. Princeton: Princeton University Press,
4 Davenport, TRH. *South Africa: A Modern History*. 1989. Bergvlei: Southern Book Publishers. See also Eldredge, EA. *Power in Colonial Africa: Conflict and Discourse in Lesotho 1870–1960*. 2007. Madison: University of Wisconsin Press.
5 Mkhonto, S. 'Black tax: A responsibility, not a burden'. News24, 20 April 2018, see https://www.news24.com/MyNews24/black-tax-a-responsibility-not-a-burden-20180419.

The burden of black tax can only be alleviated by generational wealth

Sukoluhle Nyathi

In our everyday life, a myriad of taxes must be paid, from income tax to value-added tax. This quickly became apparent to me when I received my first pay cheque, which was dramatically reduced by the amount that had to be paid to the government.

As the famous saying by English dramatist Christopher Bullock goes: ''Tis impossible to be sure of anything but death and taxes.' Of course, tax evasion comes with serious consequences and it has been the downfall of many individuals.

For black professionals like me, there is an additional tax whose burden cannot be evaded. That is, so-called black tax.

So many things with 'black' in their names are undesirable. Think blackmail. Blackface. Blacklist. However, in the context of black tax, it largely denotes that this tax is mostly incurred by black people.

The fact that it is described as a tax implies that the person subjected to it is obliged to pay. It is therefore no surprise that this term has gained a negative connotation. This, even though for many individuals the actual act of taking care of dependents is a positive practice.

While you won't necessarily find the term 'black tax' in an

economic textbook, it is increasingly popping up in African vocabulary and it is a real factor in the budgetary considerations of black South Africans. It's a recent phenomenon, with many conflicting and contradictory meanings. Here are a few key definitions and associations I got from urbandictionary.com:

- Black tax is the extra money that black professionals are expected to give every month to support their less fortunate family and extended family.
- The burden of black tax causes financial distress to middle class professionals, as they usually have no savings left after having to share their salaries with the entire family.
- There is a notion that black people have to work and perform twice as well as white people to support immediate and extended families.

The above definitions and explanations offer many insights into what black tax is and how it functions. For instance, in the first definition 'extra money' refers to any surplus or money that could otherwise be saved. The lack of a culture of saving in South Africa has often been condemned. Many households are unable to save because their disposable income is spent on financial obligations, including black tax and to service debt.

Even so, I think it's an unfair indictment to say that black households do not save at all. The proliferation of stokvels and grocery clubs is evidence of a culture of saving, even at the lowest income strata. Research has shown that there are 421 000 stokvels in the country with a membership base of

8.6 million individuals. The drawback with these savings pools is that they are channelled towards consumption as opposed to investment.

In terms of the frequency of black tax payments, they usually take place once a month. It is supposed to be a regular and consistent form of support. It is often paid in cash with the amount depending on the needs of the family or how much the benefactor can afford.

Where support is needs-based and dictated by the beneficiaries, benefactors may overextend themselves to meet their obligations. The demands may also exceed their disposable income, in which case they may be forced to borrow to meet the shortfall. Where the benefactor determines the amount, it will be based on their disposable income and may vary from month to month depending on their expenditure.

In reality 'black tax' payments aren't always done on a monthly basis. The act of caring for family members can also bring additional and often unexpected financial obligations.

For example, a death in a family is usually an unplanned-for event with unforeseen financial implications. When my cousin passed away two years ago, she had no funeral policy and was also not a member of a burial society. We all had to share the burden to ensure that her body was repatriated and that she was properly laid to rest.

Black tax need not be a series of cash payments. Take for example the child who builds or buys his parents a new home as a big, once-off gesture. Another may decide to renovate a family home or make extensions to it. However, this brings other costs, such as rates and taxes and utility payments for which they may also be held responsible. Someone who buys their parents a car may also be compelled to pay the insurance and car services.

The thing is, 'black tax' isn't a single, uniform phenomenon and the way in which it manifests will be influenced by the standard of living and income of the benefactor. Moreover, expectations will also differ from one household to another.

Family is a very important concept in the African culture. In most white families a household will typically consist of four people, i.e. a mom and dad with two kids. In a black household it is not uncommon to find eight people living in one household. In the first definition, 'extended family' therefore means this support is often extended to beyond the immediate family.

So, instead of just taking care of your parents, it can also be expected of you to look after your parents' family. The burden of dependents is increased if their children, your cousins, are in need of help, even if they don't reside in your homestead. As such, it becomes difficult, if not impossible, to limit the number of additional dependents. This is where the concept of ubuntu starts permeating the conversation because in African culture you will be condemned if you do not use your individual success to uplift others in your family.

The object of black tax is those who are 'less fortunate'. Now the reason we have less fortunate people in our society is inequality in terms of opportunities and wealth distribution. South Africa remains one of the most unequal societies in the world, with glaring disparities between the rich and the poor.

From time immemorial policies have been formulated to eradicate poverty. Whenever discussions on poverty eradication arise, I think of the the words of Jesus in John 12:8: 'The poor you will always have with you.' Should we simply accept that we cannot rid society of poverty or should we at least try to alleviate the plight of the poor? This implies that we need to give and be generous to the less fortunate in our society, but then the question becomes, can we do so consistently and in a sustained way?

Research indicates that 'black tax' is one of the main causes of financial distress amongst the South African middle-class population. The household debt-to-income ratio stands at 71.90 per cent. For this reason, 'black tax' is described as a burden. Still, people continue making these payments, willingly or begrudgingly, because they understand that it may have tragic consequences for them if they ignore the call to help, since most of time, their family members have no other form of support.

The reference to 'middle class' should also be investigated. Firstly, I feel the exclusion of the working class from the conversation about 'black tax' is unfair because they, too, carry this burden. Secondly, many black South African professionals who can boast of having attained the middle class label are in real terms just one pay cheque away from poverty.

In white communities you often find talk of generational wealth and passing on a financial legacy to the next generation. There is investment in businesses that will generate an income not only to sustain the current generation but the one that comes after it.

Black people mostly have to work twice as hard because they enter a world where the playing field is not level. The legacy of slavery, colonisation and apartheid robbed many black people of their generational wealth. These campaigns were violent, resulting in the dispossession of and oppression of black people.

Black people's participation in the economy was only as a form of cheap labour. They lost the opportunity to create and have wealth in perpetuity, because they lost the quintessential tool to establish lasting wealth – land ownership. In many African countries, as in South Africa, black people were moved to unproductive land and were given communal tenure during colonial times. Even in the rural areas, where a modicum of land ownership was available, they had lost the cultural and economic memory to perpetuate and develop their civilisation in a more progressive and holistic way.

Take the Frontier Wars, for example, where the Xhosa tirelessly fought the English for more than a hundred years. They lost the battle when they lost their food security because they killed their cattle on the instruction of the prophetess Nongqawuse. They ultimately lost their land to the colonial authorities and, from then on, the only way for them to earn a living was to ask for work from the new owners of the land and the cattle, the white people. They had to give up their own cultural and economic ways and were forced into employment, working themselves to the bone and retiring with a paltry pension.

Even those who succeeded, like the Mfengus of the late 19th and early 20th century, were despised by the white government, who didn't like it that progressive black farmers were outshining their white counterparts. So they introduced various laws and taxes on black people that culminated in the Native Land Act of 1913, which allowed the white government to confiscate black land without compensation, thus again forcing black people to be cheap labourers on the mines and farms.

Furthermore, house ownership for black South Africans was unknown outside the rural areas. This is why black households had very little or nothing to bequeath to the next generation. In the event of a parent's death the estate is usually shared equally amongst the children. However, in some cultures, the practice of male inheritance favours men because they will carry the family line.

Consider the establishment of Orlando Township in 1931. It was the first suburb in what became known as the South Western Townships (Soweto). Tiny, matchbox houses with inadequate sewerage systems were built, but only for rental tenure. Once again, the laws systematically excluded black people from participating in the housing market.

Consequently, their biggest (and often only) form of investment was – and, to an extent, still is – in cattle. It was used to put children through school, for traditional rituals and as a store of wealth. That is why even today, cattle are often regarded as having such important exchange value by black people. But it's a delicate or volatile currency because cattle are vulnerable to diseases and drought.

Till this day, housing ownership remains a contentious issue. It is easier to get car finance than housing finance. Black South Africans are lucky if they own one home in their lifetime. The majority will eventually return to their rural homes, which is often why you see a mass exodus during the major holidays, as people head off to the villages to build their retirement homes on their family homestead and pay homage to their families.

Whilst black people have historically only been able to invest in cattle, their white counterparts have had other investment vehicles to consider, like shares and stock options or bonds. In 2017, black ownership of listed companies on the Johannesburg Stock Exchange (JSE) was estimated to be 23 per cent; however, only ten per cent of this was direct investment and the balance was through indirect ownership through pension funds.

The fancy billboards advertising retirement estates in coastal towns or exclusive suburbs rarely show black couples. This is because they are not the target market. Black people rarely look at retirement homes, because they cannot afford to save for them due to black tax and a lack of a good financial start in life, which is often provided through generational wealth.

Another burden on black professionals is the phenomenon of dual households. The influx of migrant workers into the city in search of job opportunities was the cause of this. The miners lived in hostels with no amenities which were not designed to accommodate families. Families were separated and a system created where the breadwinner's earnings were split between his primary and secondary residence. So began the remittance of money to support your family back home in the Eastern Cape, Limpopo or KwaZulu-Natal.

This is replicated on a larger scale with migrant workers coming from as far afield as Nigeria, Somalia, the Democratic Republic of Congo and Zimbabwe to work in South Africa. The influx of foreigners into cities like Johannesburg, Durban and Cape Town is purely because they are in search of economic opportunities that can generate income to support their families back home.

Thousands of US dollars are remitted to Zimbabwe through official banking channels each year. These remittances also represent a kind of 'black tax'. They show how this obligation goes beyond provincial and national borders.

Most African cultures have an unwritten rule that it is your responsibility to take care of your parents in their old age. In our culture, the biggest investment you can make in life is to have children.

Our parents, like their parents, believe that your children *are* the retirement plan, and that, therefore, is non-negotiable. It is considered imprudent to have only one child because they might die or the 'investment' may not yield returns if the child is not successful in life. This investment, of course, also requires a long incubation period before it starts yielding returns.

For most black parents an education is deemed the ultimate gift you can give your child as many of them never got an education or, if they did, it was a struggle. So, an education is the biggest legacy that can be bequeathed to a child. It is often seen as a licence for the child to go into the world and earn a living which will eventually allow them to take care of their parents. In some instances, it is expected of them to contribute towards educating other siblings.

It is different for white families, especially in South Africa. Almost all of them can afford domestic care to look after their children, thanks to either generational wealth or to their being the third or fourth educated professional in their families. So even the burden of raising their children is lessened by black workers who, in most instances, have to leave their own children at home where they are vulnerable to the social ills in townships. Thus, the vicious cycle of poverty and underdevelopment is perpetuated.

When one considers the issue of 'black tax', you also have to take the role of religion in black communities into account. On the one hand, the church is criticised for being the biggest tool of colonisation. On the other hand, it is perceived as having brought enlightenment.

Whatever your views are, religion is often used to prop up the practice of black tax. Here are just two verses from the Bible that explicitly support the practice:

- 1 Timothy 5:8: 'But if anyone does not provide for his relatives and especially members of the household, he has denied the faith and is worse than an unbeliever.'
- Colossians 3:20: 'Children, obey your parents in everything, for this pleases the Lord.'

Apart from such religious motivations, ancestral beliefs also proclaim that your ancestors will bless you more if you look after your clan members.

It is also against this background that the black child carries the burden of black tax. In its benevolent form, it is a demonstration of gratitude to your bloodline, especially your parents.

In such instances it would be best to call it a benevolent tax, because it is paid willingly. Those making the contributions don't mind the sacrifice – as long as their family is well taken care of, they are happy. After all, how can you live in a mansion when your parents live in a shack? Or how do you cruise in a Mercedes-Benz when your mother gets wet in the rain waiting for a taxi?

Yet, the flipside of this is the resentful adult who has had to sacrifice buying a house for themself because they had to build one for their parents. We all know that guy who had to delay getting married and having a family of his own because he was still taking care of his parents and siblings. We all know that lady who drives a Fiat and lives in a one-bedroomed apartment, not because she can't afford better, but because she shares her income with her extended family. Or the man who still lives at home because he is putting two of his siblings through university.

There are so many stories out there, of dreams deferred and aspirations that are on hold because of the overriding demands of 'black tax'. So how do we minimise the negative impact associated with it, because even those who give willingly are financially strained by it?

I think the same way in which income tax is paid on a scale, the same should be done for 'black tax'. There should be a general understanding between black professionals and their families that they contribute in proportion to the amount they earn.

We cannot shirk our individual responsibility to uplift others because charity essentially begins at home. Yet, in our individual capacity, we are limited in how to address the structural inequalities that exist in our societies, which is why government intervention becomes important. The grant system is not sustainable because it creates a dependency syndrome. We need to start looking at other sustainable methods of empowering communities to generate income and wealth, whether it's through establishing agricultural cooperatives or using existing stokvels to invest in income-generating assets, such as rental property.

Most importantly, we need to be more focused on wealth creation so that we can empower future generations. Black tax can only be a temporary stopgap. If we can't find ways to create generational wealth, we will only continue to pass the legacy of dependency from one generation to the next.

SUKOLUHLE NYATHI was born, bred and educated in Bulawayo and currently resides in Johannesburg. An analyst by profession, she has spent almost 15 years working in various capacities in the finance and economic development sphere. A writer by passion, she has published two novels, *The Polygamist and The Gold Diggers*, the latter of which was longlisted for the Barry Ronge Fiction Award in 2019.

Black millennials don't have it all wrong

Mzuvukile Maqetuka

Just the other day, I was in a coffee shop and seated not far from a group of millennials who were talking rather loudly about black tax. Most of them were quite vocal about how abhorrent this practice was. They felt black tax impoverished them and hamstrung their personal economic development. Black South Africans came up with this practice to their detriment, they were saying.

I was intrigued by their debate. It made me think about the way in which we define this concept and also how different generations react to it.

The term 'black tax' is bandied about widely today. In its most basic definition, it refers to the expectation that black professionals should contribute financially to help struggling family members. In modern-day South Africa, it also manifests itself in young professionals dumping their children on their parents and expecting the old folks to look after them because they need to act as breadwinners.

What has become clear in recent years is that people don't feel the same way about black tax and that there is a growing unease with it, especially amongst the younger generation. There are also some who argue that it is a result of colonialism and the system of apartheid that prevailed on our shores. Consequently, black people could not enjoy the privilege and opportunity to accumulate wealth like their white counterparts and now have to support struggling family members.

For this reason, the debate around black tax centres on the black community rather than the white populace, who are not affected by this burden – as it is described in certain quarters – or responsibility. White families have created wealth over time: they have vast investments and inheritances that will continue to cushion their children for decades to come. Until such time as their black counterparts reach this point, we will continue to live with the practice of black tax.

Looking at some of the definitions of black tax that are out there, I believe it has become necessary for us to relook at how we define this phenomenon. We also need to question whether it is correct to even describe this practice as a tax.

In an article in *Weekend Witness*, commentator Vuyelwa Mtolo writes, 'Black tax is a colloquial term for sharing your salary with family and making sure that they are well taken care of before considering taking care of yourself. It feeds an expectation that a person may be liable to carry a burden if they've studied and found a job. That expectation extends beyond immediate family to extended family as well.'[1] This is the same definition used by the Urban Dictionary.[2]

Inevitably, this means that the person who is extending help is unable to focus on their own future due to their commitments to family members.

Commentator Sifiso Mkhonto makes the point that black tax is a legacy of the apartheid system that was brought into our democracy intentionally. 'The preferential treatment given to white people directly deprived black people of the opportunity to build generational wealth. With no equal rights for black and white South Africans at that time, white South Africans were able to enter democracy with proceeds of their wealth to give to their children, while black South Africans were allowed to enter the new dawn with no financial jumpstart.'[3]

What, then, are the true, historical origins of black tax? I believe it emanates from the time when colonisation took root on our shores. It can be traced back to the time when black South Africans' land and wealth, which at the time were measured by the number of livestock they possessed, were taken away from them. During precolonial times, we as black people considered wealth in terms of livestock owned, as well as the number and size of fields we had and the food produced from those fields.

Unfortunately, fate determined that their lands would be taken from them and that foreign diseases would ravage them. Men and women would be forced to become the tillers of their new masters' lands and women started working as maids in colonial masters' homesteads.

Other, new challenges emerged. For instance, different kinds of taxes had to be paid and money became the means for survival and wealth creation. The colonised also had to learn new things – their children had to be sent to schools that were run by missionaries who worked in tandem with the new masters and, later, the government of the day.

Black people did not have any control over these changes. They just had to use their sweat and toil to survive in this changing world that was once their old country.

The burden on black people increased as a new class of masters, the farmers – represented by a combination of foreign nationalities – and new forms of repression, including racial segregation, became the order of the day. Black people had to bear the brunt of these changes and began to know poverty, deprivation and marginalisation.

Today, a vast number of black people work far from their villages in urban and peri-urban areas. Many youngsters flock to the cities and men still go off to work on the mines and in factories whilst the old are left behind in villages. There, they patiently wait for remittances from those who are earning salaries and wages. It is these remittances that educate those still at school; living with their grannies in the villages and dorpies.

What is clear is that black tax has deep historical roots. However, after we've established its origins in history, instead of it making us morose, we should rather try to develop strategies to alleviate the pressure it places on individuals.

This brings me back to that day in the coffee shop when I heard the group of millennials. I couldn't help but wonder what kinds of families they came from – well-to-do or poor; traditional or urban? Later, I came to the conclusion that they might have come from any of the above and that this was rather a generational matter. In my experience, people of a much older generation do not have such debates.

As I see it, this group forms a substantial part of those who are engaging critically with this 'new' tax system and are viewing it either as a responsibility or a burden. They are educated professionals with jobs, who are expected to support their families and relatives.

According to an online portal called The Young Independents, a millennial is 'a young individual grindin' and hustlin' to make it in life. A millennial is deeply integrated within the online clickable culture . . . 56% of millennials won't even accept jobs from companies that ban social media.'[4]

I do not want to isolate this group within the discussion about black tax, but I do believe that the most vigorous debate will come from them rather than from those 'born before technology' (the BBTs). That is not to say that all millennials are critical of black tax.

These millennials seem to know what it feels like to be the product of parents who lived and struggled through apartheid. To quote The Young Independents again, 'A South African millennial understands the scars of our nation, and the frustration to break that cycle of oppression. A millennial sees beyond the conventional, and is compelled to push at these very boundaries. A millennial is willing to recreate a new, free, non-judgmental world where the colour of your skin or your gender, no longer determines the heights of success that you can reach.'

They are not as naive as the BBTs might think. The millennials, who are influenced greatly by modern technology like television and the internet, have developed a wider view of the world compared to the older generation, most of whom are stuck with what they were taught through oral history.

They do not simply accept things but challenge the status quo. I love and adore this group for their attitude to life. Though fearless in debate, they often bring real change and give a positive spin to societal phenomenon. Just look at how they took on the government when they waged the #FeesMustFall and #RhodesMustFall campaigns.

I am a BBT who benefited from black tax when my fathers' siblings supported me with their meagre savings to help my grandparents educate me. They did not see it as a burden but as a responsibility to support their own, to support the child of their brother. I wasn't the only one in my generation who benefited in this way, there were a host of others.

One of the key questions in the debate about the pros and cons of black tax is what the money given to families is used for. This causes much of the negativity around the matter, because in some instances, the money is wasted on things it wasn't intended for. This is when those who are supposed to help their families start getting an attitude of 'it is not my responsibility' and they insist that their families fend for themselves.

In my case, as in so many others, the black tax money was put to good use – it gave me an education and helped me to become the person I am today. My grandparents would never have considered using the money for frivolous things.

South Africa has one of the highest income tax rates when compared to other countries of its size. Almost half of the salaries and wages of those who are employed goes to income tax. For most people, this creates a situation where there is little or no money to save at the end of the month. This situation is getting worse and worse. Petrol prices go up monthly, which leads to increased food prices. It is no surprise that complaints and protests are the order of the day.

To return to my original question: is it correct to call this phenomenon where black South Africans support family members black tax? I don't think so. This phenomenon is part of an evolved ethical system that has existed for centuries and will continue to exist for many years still. I believe we need to develop a new definition free of negative connotations and one that will reflect this phenomenon's true origin, cause and real intention.

For this reason, I believe we should call it Collective Family Responsibility (CFR).

The debate around Collective Family Responsibility will continue until such time as South Africa has drastically reduced its rate of unemployment, increased its levels of income generation and established an effective education system where those who graduate from universities and colleges will actually find a job. Only when all of South Africa's adult citizens have a job, will all families be self-sufficient and will no one feel the 'burden of black tax'.

Only then will there no longer be a need for Thandiswa to support the more than three siblings who are being looked after by grandma and grandpa. Only then will she be in a position to use any extra money in the month to build her own wealth and can her parents or grandparents use their social grant for what it was meant for.

MZUVUKILE MAQETUKA was born in 1952 in Graaff-Reinet. After school, he enrolled for a degree in economics and accounting at the University of Fort Hare. Unable to finish his studies as a result of his involvement in student politics through the South African Students' Organisation (SASO), he went into exile in 1979. In 1991 he completed his studies at the University of Westminster in London, where he obtained a BA (Hons) degree in Photography, Film and Video Production.

Notes

1 Mtolo, V. 'Living with black tax', *Weekend Witness*, 19 March 2018, see https://www.news24.com/SouthAfrica/News/living-with-black-tax-20180316.

2 See https://www.urbandictionary.com/define.php?term=Black%20 Tax.

3 Mkhonto, S. 'Black Tax: a responsibility, not a burden', News24, 20 April 2018, see https://www.news24.com/MyNews24/black-tax-a-responsibility-not-a-burden-20180419.

4 Author unknown. 'What is a South African millennial?' on The Young Independents, see https://www.tyi.co.za/your-life/news/what-is-a-south-african-millennial-7140503.

Sacrificing the self for the whole

Lidudumalingani

1.

Even before you are born, the path of your life has already been mapped. It goes on and on and then it turns on itself and goes into a loop. There are days when you feel dizzy from travelling around in circles.

On some days, it feels like foreign objects have been placed on your path for no other reason than to inconvenience you. You do not notice the first thousand tumbles. You dismiss the dirt on your clothes as the residue of nightmares you cannot fully recall.

The lump in your throat, it must be from the nightmare. A chant you cannot remember singing. You begin to feel exhausted. It becomes clear that the world is not kind to a dark-skinned and poor person. You have tried it. This thing of being positive, seeing the silver lining; except sometimes, there is no silver lining in sight.

2.

This is how black tax begins . . . It doesn't start when you are much older and have a job, with endless siblings to support and ageing parents who have no pension whom you must look after. No, it already begins to eat at you at the mall when your father tells you the sneakers you want are too expensive to buy. You are twelve. You stare at him in disappointment and then you stare at the sneakers again. You can hear them call your name.

From that day, you make a promise to yourself that, for the sake of your wellbeing, you will suppress your desires. You also naively make the promise that when you are older and more successful than your dad – which you will be, you promise yourself – you will buy yourself all the sneakers in the world.

It does not occur to you at that moment in the store, when you notice the absence of meat at dinner or when you are told you can't attend the school's outing because there is no money, that this is the path your life will take for the remainder of your days on this earth. That you will come to know these shortcomings intimately, like one comes to know the limits of their own love.

Throughout your childhood, there are the glimpses of another life, an alternative universe, where you are sitting in a mansion, perhaps floating in a jacuzzi, driving down a highway, air blowing through your thick hair, and you are wearing the sneakers your parents could not afford to get you. Depending on what day it is, these glimpses are more or less frequent. They are always a distraction that rescues you from the abyss you are destined for.

When you get to Kwebulana Junior Secondary School, a school in the small town of Tsomo in the Eastern Cape, nothing sets you apart from the other children. With a few exceptions, all the children in your village, called Zikhovane, go to the same school. They steal each other's jerseys because they know their parents cannot afford one. But you do not steal. You choose to stay cold until your father buys you a jersey.

Given the tiny steps you take, no longer than a few inches, it takes 40 minutes to get to school and another 40 minutes back. The journey is split into two equal halves, separated by a river. Twenty minutes after leaving home, you dip into the river, home falling out of view, and then from the riverbank, it takes 20 more minutes to get to school.

On the days that it rains nonstop, the fields you walk through to get to school swallow your shoes. The earth is hungry – the soil is soft from years of planting. You stick your hand in, grab the shoe, and drag it out in a twirling movement. Now you have mud for a shoe.

When you leave primary school to attend high school at Tsomo Junior Secondary School, the differences between you and the other children are more starkly outlined. The school tracksuit – the official winter wear – costs more than your parents can afford. And so, in winter you put on a few kilograms when you wear other jerseys underneath the school jersey to stay warm. As soon as the weather becomes warmer you lose this 'weight' again without doing any exercise, by simply shedding jerseys.

You start to wonder why you were placed on this earth. Surely, you tell yourself, this is not by God's design, it must be by someone else's design. This is the first time that you think about suicide.

3.

While attending a soccer match in the next village, Hange, you run into your uncle. The one who never stops talking – not at a full stop, not at the end of a thought.

Your uncle tells you that he cannot read. You know this, everyone does. He tells you why he cannot read and also explains why your father never went to school. He says your father's education was interrupted by the same thing as his. Your father was 18 when the The Employment Bureau of Africa (TEBA) recruiters came for boys his age to take them to the mines as labour. It was deep in the apartheid years then.

All it took to pass the test to work in the mines was the ability to stand up straight, cough up no blood and hold your arms above your head without grimacing. Your father has been working all his life in the mines, yet he still is not being paid the money he is worth. The life of the black man is such.

It breaks your heart. The consequences of apartheid and cheap migrant labour have travelled, like the gold mines that stretch for many kilometres underground, all the way from the mining town of Sasolburg to meet you right here in this moment.

You think again of that episode at the store, and all the other stores, the tracksuit, the school outings missed. You had started to ask your parents for less and less each day until you stopped asking altogether. If you couldn't borrow it, you went without, and you were fine with it, or pretended to be.

It was then that you changed your thinking about driving down a highway, air blowing through your thick hair. Now you wanted to get a job so you could send money home. And thus it began. The joy of it . . . the burden of it. Black tax.

It occurs to you that black tax was always a thing in your family. Your father went to work in the mines at 18 to feed the rest of the family and in a way you were destined to follow the same path, even if slightly different.

Your path will come with the illusion of an education. It is a key to success, they tell you, one that will unlock all doors, imaginary and otherwise.

By the time matric comes, you have changed your mind about what you want to be so many times that there are not many options left. Each time you look up a new field of study, you realise your parents will not be able to afford it and so your career choice is based on how much your parents can pay, not on what you want to study. Despite their good intentions, it does not help that your teachers keep telling you that you are smart and that one day you will make a highly successful accountant.

You take a gap year after passing matric with distinction, in the hope that it will give you time to remap your life. You work at a local supermarket to save up some money for university. But after that year, you still don't know what you want to be and what you want to study.

You enrol for the cheapest course at Walter Sisulu University. There, you share a tiny flat with three other students whose habits you detest. One of them never flushes the toilet properly. The other eats food that is left in the fridge without first checking to whom it belongs.

You work on weekends. You never sleep. You never ask your parents for a cent. You tell them you are fine. You are always fine.

Unlike primary and secondary school, at university it becomes clear that you are not like the other children, but now, luckily, your will is stronger, and so you live within your means, sending money home when you can.

4.

You are now an adult, or trying to be one. On most days, you curse the idea of it, but you are here now and after all, you have wanted it your entire life. As a child, you desired to be an adult and to be exempt from restricting curfews, mapped sleeping and a television schedule.

Here you are then. The adult you have always wanted to be.

You move from job to job and in each you negotiate a raise, always at least R3 000 or more. You tell your parents about every job move and spare no details. You tell them how much you are earning now, how many people work at your new company, how many of them are female, black, your age, older – you even tell them the directions to your place of work, although they have never set foot in Johannesburg.

The conversation is carried on the kind of laughter that comes from the belly. Voices rise and drop in a calculated rhythm. It is the kind of laughter that you only share with your parents. Each conversation ends, the laughter still carrying it, and then the list of demands comes. Your mother wants to renovate the old house by the gate. It is not pretty when you enter the yard, she tells you. Nobody uses mats anymore, she says, all the houses need tiles. And there where the small flat is, she wants to build a bigger house, with enough bedrooms to accommodate a small village.

When you are back in the city and looking for a new flat,

you enter a lower maximum amount, but you like nothing that comes up. You book a viewing for a flat in a quiet area where there are fewer blocks of flats. The fewer the people, the quieter the block will be, you say. It justifies the price, you convince yourself.

At month end, you send your mother the money for the tiles and the new bedroom. Every month, there is always something else, always costing a little more than the previous month.

In the months that you do not send any money two things happen: your parents call to ask what you think they will be eating; they also tell you that because of your non-contribution that month, they cannot go to a relative's umgidi to compensate for the gifts they received from them when they sent you to school.

And then the WhatsApps dry up. Your mother stops sending you Bible verses on every day of the week. She stops telling you what trouble your aunt, who is always involved with some married man, has done that week.

You want to know if everything is fine with them, but you are reluctant to ask. So, you wait it out. A few weeks later, you make the call, reluctantly and upset.

This call and the subsequent calls, until you send some money home, begins or ends with 'Siyalamba apha,' we are hungry here. Sometimes you say how some money will be deposited into your account within the next few days and that you will send her some. On other days, you hang up without saying a word.

As a joke, to temporarily relieve all your aching parts, you post on social media that there is too much month at the end of your money. The message notifications collide as they come in on your phone, interrupting each other's urgency. All of them are from sympathisers, who are also in the grips of black tax.

You are careful not to post on your WhatsApp story. Once, you spent an entire morning explaining to your mother how it works and since then she has posted so many Bible verses that she could start a whole new religion. You call your parents, moments after baring your heart to the universe, and tell them that the money has been deposited, but that it will only reflect in your bank account after three working days.

That evening, your empty fridge rattles in the background, louder than usual. It does not take long for the two-minute noodles to be ready. You empty three packets into a pot, the meat in the fridge is for lunch.

One weekend, you while away the time at home, sleeping and binge-watching a TV series you have already seen countless times. The opening sequence is the soundtrack of your life. You track the characters with precision and wonder why some had to die and another had to marry the one character you like the least. It reminds you of lovers who refused to watch the series with you or others who did, but fell asleep or dared to get up to answer a phone call.

At the end of another spell of light sleep, you cannot make out if it is afternoon or morning. It only matters in as far as it tracks your own existence, tells you whether you are alive or not. The light trickles through the curtains to tell you what time it is. It is definitely not evening yet, because the lights are not on yet.

The bedroom you are watching the series from is engulfed in depressing darkness. Only the flashing light of the laptop battles the dark. The rest of the room has succumbed to it. Only the edges of things can be seen. You have no plans for the weekend and no intention to leave the flat.

The next weekend, after sending home all of the money from a consulting job, you are left with just enough to carry you until the end of the month, but then you remember a friend's birthday is coming up. He created a WhatsApp group for it, on which someone suggests an expensive restaurant in an upmarket area. Everybody nods, thumbs up, as it goes on WhatsApp.

You wait for someone to point out that it is not month end and that the dinner should be moved to a far less expensive place. You're quite sure at the other end of the group, someone is pacing up and down, also praying that someone will suggest this. The double ticks, the signal that someone is writing, haunt you. At the end, nobody speaks up.

So, the Saturday night arrives, with reservations made at the expensive place. Luckily it is not far from your flat and the Uber won't cost more than R20 a trip. The meal gives you nightmares – the fucker can easily add up to R500 and so you transfer a little bit of money from your savings. Only for tonight, you say, staring at your judgemental banking app.

You leave behind your smell on the seats of the Uber, traces of your presence, of your dripping sauce, of ukunyisa. The night is everything it is meant to be. Your friend says he is so happy to celebrate his big day with close friends. There are tears of joy.

The meal is expensive, close to the R500 you had 'budgeted' – how laughable.

Along with the notification of the transfer comes an urgent

SMS from your younger sibling. They need data and money for airtime. Older siblings who have a job cannot not have money and so you transfer whatever was left from what you had set aside for the birthday celebrations. You need to keep up appearances as the older sibling who is everyone's favourite because love flows unlimitedly through their bank account.

The leftover wine from the dinner calls your name. You drink it to sleep, like others drink sleeping pills. In the morning, your nose draws its smell from the glass you did not finish. One gulp and it is finished, swallowed whole with the flaky dust that floats on top of the wine.

That Sunday is a day to sulk, to remember a job that brings no joy, no money. It is a day to think of black tax and the ways in which its hands extend to your bank account and your soul, wreaking havoc.

You dive into the series you are watching even before opening the curtains and by the afternoon, you remember there is laundry that needs to be done. You drag your body out of bed, you put the laundry in and retreat to bed. To your series. To the soundtrack of your misery.

Another bank notification beeps. At month end, your sibling at university needs to make the required quarterly payments. Somehow, this slipped the minds of your parents when they were busy spending the money you had sent only a few days ago on tiles, pillows and new curtains. Then there are the groceries for your mother and the labour building the new house that need to be paid for.

The thought of all of this, in addition to your rent, car instalment, car insurance, phone, DStv, electricity and petrol put you to sleep. You drift in and out of consciousness.

A friend has given birth to their second child and they send you a photo of the baby wrapped in a blanket with flowers. You send a heart emoji. It is all you can do; your money is already stretched beyond its limits. You realise if you were to have a child now, you would have to feed them with prayers and clothe them in dreams. The thought leaves your mind faster than it entered – it is not wanted here.

Tomorrow it is back to work again, you sink into a state of temporary depression.

The morning arrives and you cry after stepping out of the shower. There is no motivation to leave the flat and go to work. You get dressed whilst shaking from the sobs. The clothes slip onto you reluctantly, your shirt buttons are mixed up and your jersey is caught by something and does not wrap around your neck. You will be late for work, so you tell your clothes to fuck off and you call yourself an idiot.

At last you leave the house, first to face the traffic and then work; to work for a salary that is not enough to last until month end.

Every day of your life you go round and round in circles, because the path of your life has been mapped for you, long before you were born. Your only job is to negotiate the terms of how you follow it.

LIDUDUMALINGANI is an award-winning writer, photographer and filmmaker. He is the 2016 winner of the Caine Prize for African Writing and a recipient of the Miles Morland Scholarship.